W0028450

CHALK STREAMS & LAZY TROUT

· *Pictured by a Trout Fisherman* ·

Robin Armstrong

Foreword by Sir Michael Hordern

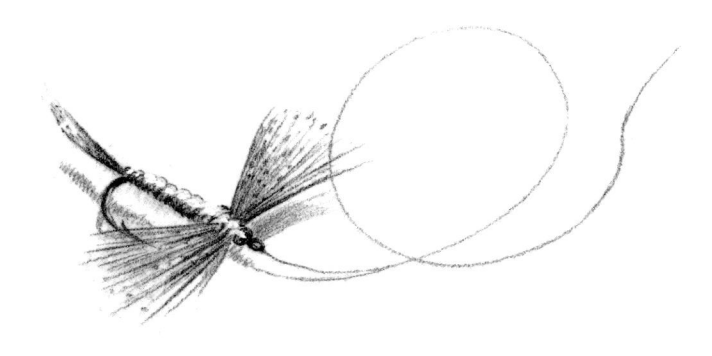

STANLEY PAUL
London Sydney Auckland Johannesburg

*To all anglers who practise care and concern
for our precious rivers and in particular those who nurture
our chalk streams*

Acknowledgements

I should like to thank the following people for helping and supporting me in the preparation of this book:

Dermot Wilson, to whom every angler should be grateful; Rags Locke (the grayling man); Fred Buller for his encouragement in the early days; Marion Paull and Roddy Bloomfield for being so patient; Guy Robinson for allowing me access to the great Leckford water to sketch; Colonel Ian McCausland, Sir Ian Aisher and the Orvis company for help in allowing me fishing days; Tricia Haye for restoring and maintaining my confidence; and last but certainly not least, Bob Speddy.

Woodtown, March, 1991

Stanley Paul & Co. Ltd
An imprint of the Random Century Group
20 Vauxhall Bridge Road, London SW1V 2SA

Random Century Australia (Pty) Ltd
20 Alfred Street, Milsons Point, Sydney, NSW 2061

Random Century New Zealand Limited
PO Box 40–086, Glenfield, Auckland 10

Century Hutchinson South Africa (Pty) Ltd
PO Box 337, Bergvlei 2012, South Africa

First published 1991
Copyright © Robin Armstrong 1991

The right of Robin Armstrong to be identified as the author of this work has been asserted by him in accordance with the Copyright, Designs and Patents Act, 1988

Set in Century Old Style by Tek Art Ltd,
Addiscombe, Croydon, Surrey

Colour reproduction by Colorlito, Milan, Italy

Printed and bound in Great Britain by
Butler and Tanner Ltd, Frome, Somerset

All rights reserved

A catalogue record for this book is available
from the British Library

ISBN 0 09 174210 2

· Contents ·

	Foreword	6
	Preface	7
	Introduction	8
1	*FONS ET ORIGO*	9
2	THE NOBLE TROUT	14
3	*PRIMUS INTER PARES*	19
4	HALFORD'S RIVER	25
5	THE QUADRILATERAL	35
6	THE KIMBRIDGE BEAT	39
7	THE UPPER AVON	46
8	MATCHING THE HATCH	54
9	AUTUMN GLORY	60
10	CHALK STREAM AND CHERRYBROOK	66
11	RIVERSIDE DIVERSIONS	72
12	VICTORIANA AND THE CULT OF THE 'DRAY-FLAY'	77
13	FUTURE CONDITIONAL	84
	Tailpiece	92

Halford's tackle

WHAT shall we see, as we look across the broad, still, clear river, where the great dark trout sail to and fro lazily in the sun? For having free-warren of our fancy and our paper, we may see what we choose.

White chalkfields above, quivering hazy in the heat. A park full of merry haymakers; gay red and blue waggons; stalwart horses switching off the flies; dark avenues of tall elms; groups of abele, 'tossing their whispering silver to the sun;' and amid them the house. What manner of house shall it be? Tudor or Elizabethan, with oriels, mullioned windows, gables, and turrets of strange shape? No; that is commonplace. Everybody builds Tudor houses now. Our house shall smack of Inigo Jones or Christopher Wren; a great square red-brick mass, made light and cheerful though by quoins and windows of white Sarsen stone; with high-peaked French roofs, broken by louvres and dormers, haunted by a thousand swallows and starlings. Old walled gardens, gay with flowers, shall stretch right and left. Clipt yew alleys shall wander away into mysterious gloom; and out of their black arches shall come tripping children, like white fairies, to laugh and talk with the girl who lies dreaming and reading in the hammock there, beneath the black velvet canopy of the great cedar-tree, like some fair Tropic flower hanging from its boughs. Then they shall wander down across the smooth-shorn lawn, where the purple rhododendrons hang double, bush and image, over the water's edge, and call to us across the stream, 'What sport?' and the old Squire shall beckon the keeper over the long stone bridge, and return with him bringing luncheon and good ale; and we will sit down, and eat and drink among the burdock leaves, and then watch the quiet house, and lawn, and flowers, and fair human creatures, and shining water, all sleeping breathless in the glorious light beneath the glorious blue, till we doze off, lulled by the murmur of a thousand insects, and the rich minstrelsy of nightingale and blackcap, thrush and dove.

Charles Kingsley: CHALKSTREAM STUDIES

· *Foreword* ·

O PEN the leaves of this book at random and no page but instructs with the pen or enchants with the brush.

I have fished with the author and shared his waterside appreciations – a keeper, a writer, a fisherman, an artist – *Rara Avis*, this Robin.

Michael Hordern

· *Preface* ·

*C*HALK STREAMS & LAZY TROUT is a wildlife artist's collation of random thoughts and pictures on the subject of fly fishing and some of the people associated with that delicate art as practised on the chalk streams of southern England, particularly the River Test.

Gentle and limpid, utterly charming and seductive, the Test still meanders through the soft green meadows of Hampshire much as it has always done – modestly and deceptively, its prim, pellucid waters offering the easiest of fine trout. Until, that is, you try to take them. For this coy mistress of a river, like all chalk streams, guards her treasures more subtly than you think. Just as you are revelling in her seeming abundance, you find, as you kick yourself for forgetting, that the fish you can see so clearly can also, clearly and disdainfully, see you.

The broad valley of the Test is very lovely, and the river offers fine sport. Here as well as anywhere is the 'sweet perfection' of English rural life made manifest; it is an easy scene to celebrate. But I have not conceived these essays merely as exercises in bucolic nostalgia. While they honour the past, they also look, with varying degrees of hope and pessimism, to the uncertain future which faces both the river and the land through which it flows.

The art and craft (and science) of fly fishing is an old and tricky one, stretching back over two thousand years or so, and the path of the naturalist is strewn with hazards. If from carelessness, or sheer ignorance, I have in places erred or strayed from the path of accuracy, may the Lords of the Angle, spiritual and temporal, graciously permit me to seek pardon in advance.

One final point. I know and respect many first-class women anglers, but to add 'and fisherwomen' after every reference to a 'fisherman' would make the text unduly clumsy, while to use the word 'fisherperson' would be daft. In these pages, following an old legal convention, every 'he' should be assumed to embrace a 'she'.

· *Introduction* ·

'I LOVE any discourse of rivers, and fish and fishing,' said Walton, and most anglers share his passion. It is not enough for us to practise our art; we must also talk about it, preferably in the company of our fellows, warmed by good drink. For fishing is something more than stalking a fish, and hooking it, and playing it, and bringing it safely to the bank. It is a sport for all seasons and all manner of honest men – a philosophy even, to be argued over when midwinter weather keeps us indoors and the only bird-song to be heard is the hoot of a cold owl above a biting north-easterly.

All this is good news for writers like me, since it means that our books will stand a fair chance of being welcomed by fishermen, so long as the books themselves are well enough written and produced, and add something to the general dialogue which arises whenever two anglers meet.

I hope this volume will contribute to the ongoing discourse. Fishing, and all the pleasures which go with it, fill me with such intense joy that I burst to share my delight with a wider audience. But I do know that private enthusiasms, over-solemnly urged, can scare away those for whom the sport is no more than one pastime among many. I have therefore tried in this book to be both serious and light-hearted: serious about the future of fishing, and the countryside in which we fish; light-hearted about my own fishing experiences and minor vanities. I have also delved gently into some bits of our Victorian fishing past, since it was the Victorians, and Victorian tackle-makers, who led us to where we are now.

Because this book is about fly fishing on chalk streams, I have said something of Frederic M. Halford who, together with his friends in the Houghton Club, helped to pioneer today's version of the art. What Halford researched a hundred years ago, particularly in respect of the entomology of flies, the conservation of fish and the managing of a fishery, is still relevant to what we do, or should be doing, today.

There are two tenuous themes which run through most of these pages: the joys of fly fishing and the need, if those joys are to be passed on to the next generation, for sensible conservation. But each chapter stands on its own, and not every one will interest every reader. Any which fill you with a leaden heart may always be skipped. So long as some of them please you, and some of the paintings evoke memories of times well spent, I shall be content.

CHAPTER 1

· Fons et Origo ·

I CAME to chalk-stream fishing relatively late and relatively ignorant. I had read about it, and aspired to it, but it always escaped me until I began to make friends who lived in chalk-stream country. And that country was quite unlike my usual beats: it was softer, gentler and more predictable, with an underlying geomorphology very different from the harsh granites of Dartmoor, my other hunting ground. It seemed that I needed to know a lot more about the nature of its placid streams if I was to fish them with any success.

From what I read and see, much of surface-green Hampshire and Wiltshire is underpinned in whitest white. Dig carefully into many parts of the natural turf and you will find you can fashion a distinctive White Horse, or a rude Long Man which can be seen from miles away. In everyday terms the white is chalk, 'an opaque, soft, earthy limestone, consisting chemically of carbonate of lime with some impurities', and it lurks beneath those gentle downs in large quantity. How it got there is an intriguing but longer story than I care to tell; sufficient that it is there and has been there for more years than most of us can imagine.

It is the chalk, not surprisingly, which governs the nature of the chalk stream, the porous rock acting like a sponge to retain water beneath the surface, releasing it slowly over a period of time. Hampshire rarely experiences the flash floods which occur on Dartmoor, where sudden rains burst out from the hills almost as fast as they fall, swelling the rivers and storming down to the sea in angry torrents. The Test and the Itchen mostly eschew such intemperate behaviour, content to let their flow be regulated naturally in a gradual discharge from the aquifer, the unseen reservoir lying below the surface of the sleepy landscape.

It is a benign and beneficent arrangement. And so long as rude industrial man does nothing awful to disrupt it, all will probably go on as it has always done. The rivers will swell and relax according to season, but never with undue haste nor cavalier excess. When the water table rises, the water will flow into the river system; streams will appear in the upper reaches, and the rate of flow in the main channels will gently increase. But let the water table fall too low, by wrongly siting boreholes, or abstracting too much water for domestic or industrial consumption, or causing the earth's crust to collapse by careless ploughing, and the rivers will be starved, excessive weed may form and the numbers of healthy trout will surely diminish.

Manipulating water sources is always a tricky business. What you do at point A can never be done without affecting what happens at point B, or even C, D, E and a hundred points more. Diverting surface water channels is chancy enough, but diverting or making excessive demands on what lies beneath the surface is an even greater shot in the dark. Years ago I remember a sheep disappearing down a well in Kent, to be washed out, days later, from a subterranean stream more than twenty miles away. No one could know where it had travelled, and no one could have foretold where it would reappear, for no one knew the courses of the underground river system which had borne it along. I suspect that a similar unpredictable system lies under much of Hampshire.

Nature, by and large, is generous and surprisingly forgiving: she will make good any small depredations or occasional excessive demands that might be made on her. But to draw too much from her munificent store, to lean too heavily on her amiable goodwill, is to court disaster. Some day, and perhaps sooner than we expect, the water table could be permanently dented and the river system ruined for ever. It is for anglers, as well as conservationists, to see that this does not happen. The price of tomorrow's fishing is vigilant monitoring of all today's slickly presented proposals to develop an environment which could all too easily be damaged irretrievably.

The chalk not only regulates the water's flow; it filters and cleans it before releasing it through the gravels which finally screen it to produce the limpid streams in which we all rejoice. These streams, though they may appear clear, abound in the dissolved nutrients which favour the growth of riverine plants. In turn, the plants then provide food for a flourishing population of the molluscs and insects which make for happy and healthy trout and contented fishermen.

But that is not the end of the matter. The ecosystem is a labyrinth of inter-dependency and inter-reaction. Many of today's river keepers even believe that the dead fish it was once customary to remove should be left to rot in the water, to nourish and fatten, in due course, the plants on which they originally depended, rather as hatless walkers on Ilkley Moor will finally feed worms to provide fodder for the ducks. Whether or not this is right, we cannot deny the infinite complexity of the world around us. We can only rejoice that the chalk stream provides a pretty comfortable living for the trout which provide our sport.

Chalk streams have other virtues. Their nutrients produce not only the right fish food, but also long and luxuriant 'streamer' weeds which give a harassed trout a sporting chance to escape even the best of anglers. No one looks for too easy a catch, and the chalk streams only rarely provide one. But what they do provide is the sort of peace and tranquillity that can make even an empty and unproductive day a happy one.

And this, perhaps, is why so many words have already been written about them in books and articles down the years. But if my modest illustrated contribution to this piscine word mountain can reach and enthuse some deprived angler who so far knows nothing of chalk-stream delights, I shall feel no guilt.

· *View of the Test from Mottisfont* ·
(overleaf)

In any competition for the most beautiful waterscape in England, a thousand scenes might vie for first place. I won't presume to judge which one would win. I simply record that when I painted this picture, I thought myself as close to heaven as I shall ever be. It was a perfect summer day: the sky was an English blue and the trees a rich green, and the bustling twentieth century was only barely discernible in the sound of a distant aeroplane. The river, as befitted one as old and honourable as this, was bright and clear. While I live, I thought, this is paradise enough; when I die, this is where I should like to make my rendezvous with the great and the good of anglers past.

Mottisfont, about 4½ miles north-west of Romsey, is a place much hallowed in the history of chalk-stream fishing. It's a safe guess that the twelfth-century founders of the Augustinian priory which once stood here took trout and salmon from the stream that still runs through the estate. It's also a safe guess that succeeding owners of the house which replaced the abbey after its dissolution continued to do the same.

But unlike modern anglers, the good monks probably relished the pike which lurked and (despite the efforts of generations of river keepers) still lurk in these waters. For pike represented good money at that time: Mrs E.M. Walker, in her *Sportsman's Cookbook*, reports that their thirteenth-century price was double that of salmon. And what the monks didn't sell they would eat, as the Germans and the French still do and Izaak Walton once did. It was a fish, he said, 'too good for any but anglers or very honest men'.

The pike are fewer than they were. So, too, are the salmon and trout, although both still spawn here. The village where Halford gave his annual dinner still exists, and the house he must have known now belongs to the National Trust, with the fishing rights let out to a large public company. As on most chalk streams, the weed is said to be over-nourished with nitrates run off from the large farms, and the fishing is regularly enhanced with well-grown brown trout, fingerlings and, in mid-season, a few rainbows. But even without fish in them these waters would gladden any man's eye, let alone an artist's.

If anyone were to propose this area for development of any sort (and the idea is not as preposterous as it may seem given the rapacity of some developers), I would suggest that he be taken from his city office and hanged from the tallest tree in Hampshire until such time as he expires miserably, and his flesh withers and his bones whiten – not because I am particularly vengeful but simply to discourage any others who might dare to suggest that they could improve on what is already a perfect combination of land and water. So let us rejoice in such treasures and guard them well.

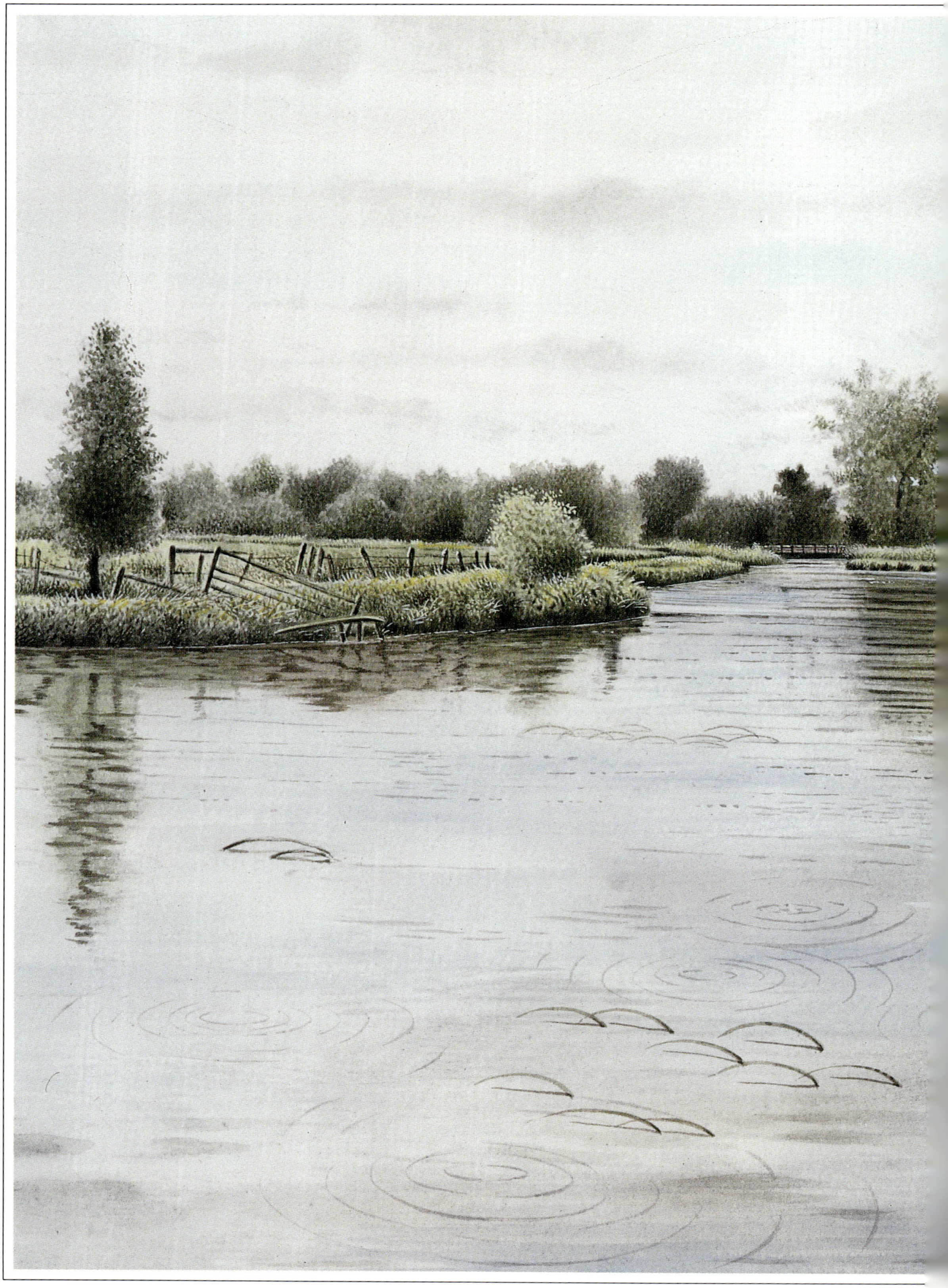

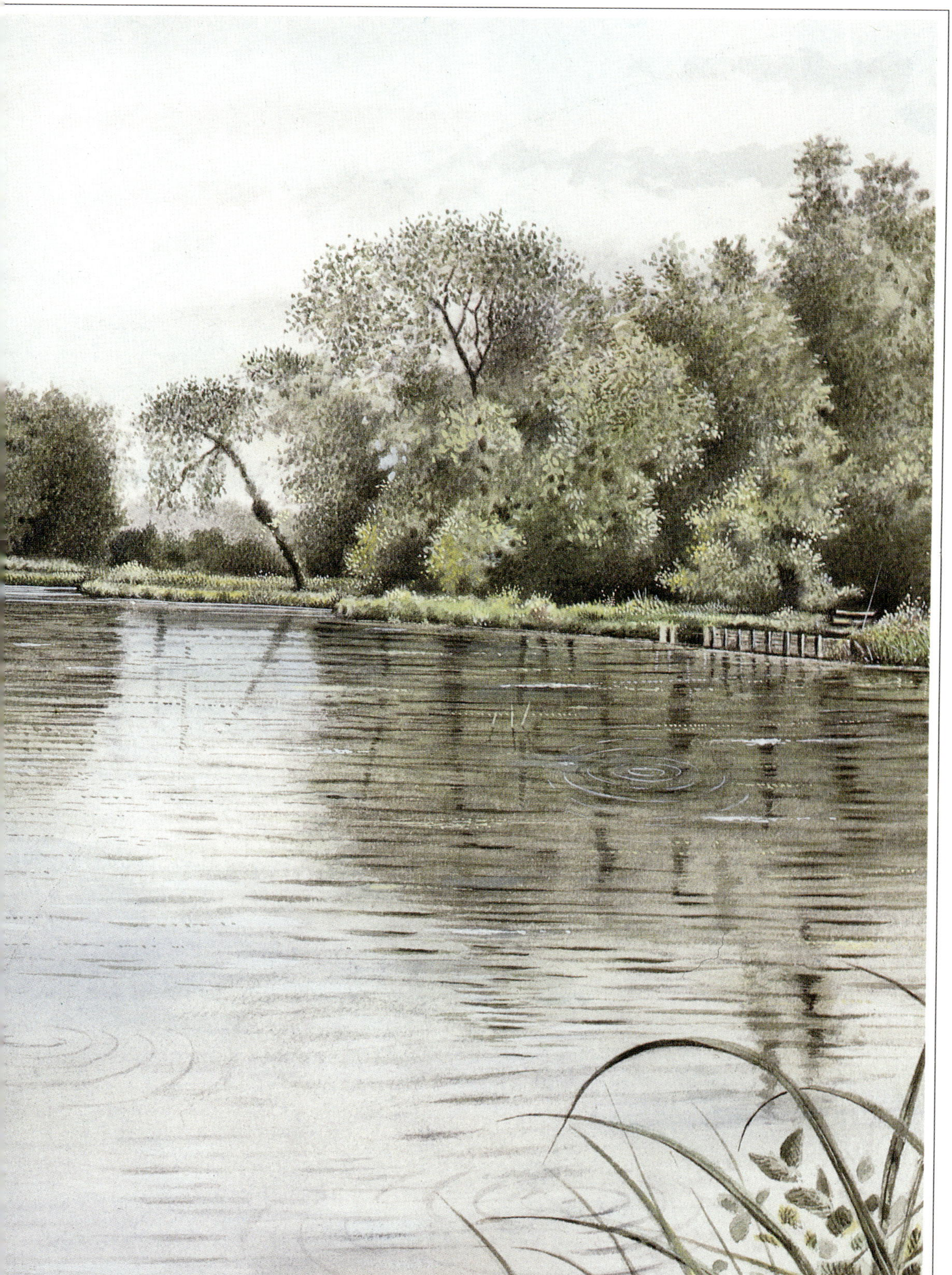

CHAPTER 2
· *The Noble Trout* ·

TROUT toil not, neither do they spin; like the lilies of the field, they are justified not by their works but by the beauty of their being. Let it be enough that they are, without asking what they do, for what they are is clear enough: a boon and a blessing to all who pursue them. Throughout those countries in which they are found, trout are acknowledged as a fisherman's delight: a source of constant wonder, and irritation; creatures which flirt and captivate then dance away, vaunting themselves and filling us all with hope, only to dash those hopes in swift and darting flight.

The joys and challenges they offer are not restricted to Britain. I have fished for them in fierce and untamed rivers in Canada and New Zealand, grilling them afterwards over hot, slow-burning wood to find them every bit as delicious as anything out of Mottisfont or the Dart. But this wide distribution doesn't mean that they are simply an indiscriminate, commonplace sort of creature. For a start, they don't relish extremes of heat and cold, and they do need an adequate supply of decent water; unlike some more tolerant breeds of fish, they cannot easily survive in rivers or canals that man has made murky.

As befits their good looks and elegance, trout are somewhat fussy about their surroundings, preferring to live in smart chalk streams or lordly, wild upland becks well away from the noise and the dirt of inner-city waterways. They thrive best in places man has not yet defiled; they like cleanliness, fresh air and a bit of space, and sporting adversaries who play the game according to proper rules. It is unlikely that fish in general (other than English fish) care much about social distinctions, but if they did they would probably acknowledge that trout belong to the upper orders of the piscine world. Even fish-farm trout, hand-reared and spoilt rotten, still retain some of their ancestral arrogance when they are finally released into the harsh world outside the stock-pond.

Like the men who fish for them, trout are remarkably cosmopolitan, at ease in very many different places from New Zealand to Nebraska, cheerfully making homes in the sombre waters of highland lochs and lowland reservoirs; in ponds and pools from Loch Ness to Lake Huron; in rivers great and small, from the brawling burns of Dartmoor to the pellucid, ordered chalk streams of Hampshire. My son's *Animal World* book shows me (as well as him) some seven different varieties of trout, hinting at many more in parts of the world neither of us have yet explored. He, predictably, likes the sound of the cut-throat trout and is intrigued by the Apache, but what really fascinate him, having been used to the brownies I bring home from the streams of the upper moor, are the figures after each picture. That average weights of different kinds of trout vary between one and five pounds, he can believe. But quoted top weights of up to fifty pounds he finds hard to swallow. 'Those fish,' he says, 'must be heavier than the boys in the infants' class.'

As so they must. I can understand him when he says he finds it hard to believe that all these different kinds and sizes of fish belong to the same salmonidae family. I am not able to enlighten him very scientifically, and content myself with drawing his attention to a piece of the text: 'To many fishermen, trout are the greatest game fishes of fresh water. Most species are wary and demand skilful fishing. When hooked, they fight hard to get free; even a small trout is fun to catch.' I then suggest, to make up for my lack of biological expertise, that trout are much like members of a Scottish clan, spread all over the globe and settled in different places, whose offspring have acquired their own special characteristics and varying lifestyles without losing their original humours.

Some, from rushing upland brooks, are small, brown and tough and very fast-moving: these are the Gurkha branch of this remarkable family. Others, born with silver spoons in their well-fed mouths on rich, lowland rivers like the Test, and blessed with a lot of nice, clear, carefully kept water in which to play, are the Chalk Stream Household Cavalry: well burnished and laid-back, yet still formidable and more than capable of fighting the good fight among the ins and outs of Hampshire weed beds.

Different again are the rainbows, originally brought into Britain from North America towards the end of the nineteenth century, and altogether plumper and more colourful than brown trout. They are not front-line fish, being too big and easy to spot and not used to the fast action needed to survive in the boulder-strewn 'pots and guts' of the hill country. But even these comfortable creatures, long used to convenience food and the rich ways of American life, soon learn to take care of themselves when they are shoved out into a fishery and left to fend for themselves. When you are sought through every seasonal hour by a crowd of keen anglers, most of whom are determined to get their daily money's worth, you quickly learn the tricks necessary for survival. It may be hard for the stream-trudging purist to admit, but many of these lake-stocked rainbows become so well seasoned in evading capture that taking them is as hard as landing any naturally reared fish.

But then, it is one of the Rules of the Universe, laid down by the gods at the beginnings of time, that there is no such thing as an easy trout. Whatever their breed or antecedents, and in whichever part of the world they are found, they all share an instinctive cunning and a sharp percipience of what man is trying to do to them. When next century's behavioural psychologists succeed in communicating with fish, they will discover only what anglers have known for centuries: that the trout's first ambition is to live until a ripe old age. It never gives up easily, and I am always moved by the ferocity with which it defends its life unto the last breath.

· *Brown trout taking a nymph near Salisbury, on the upper Avon* ·

No sensible trout is going to expose itself to the air, a dangerous element in which it is not at home, when it can perfectly well feed below the waterline on a wholesome nymph. And wholesome nymphs are rarely in short supply. Mostly, and with several provisos and caveats, aquatic flies lay their eggs on the surface, whence the eggs drift down to cling to weed at the bottom. After a year or so the eggs develop into larvae, and subsequently into naive and struggling nymphs – tubular, grub-like and desperately seeking sunlight. Frail and tiny, the successful nymph battles through current and surface tension to emerge from its grub case as a fly, ready to take to the air as soon as its wings are dry enough to support it.

Barring a miracle of research invention, what percentage of all the millions of eggs laid ever reach maturity will never be known, but it cannot be very high. Apart from the waste in eggs themselves, predators of the maturing nymph in the shape of fish and birds lie on every hand; only the tiniest portion ever survive to reach cover among the grasses of the riverbank. And even those that do reach this stage of diaphanous maturity have but a short time to live – a week at most, but more commonly a day or two. Like many beautiful creatures, they are doomed to early death. After a brief spell of ritual dancing, leading (as dancing often does) to mating, the males disappear to die happily (one assumes) on land while the female returns to the water to lay her eggs. This done, she too expires.

To an imaginative theatrical producer, the whole process would furnish (perhaps it already has) a spectacular theme for a tragic ballet. To the more prosaic fisherman it is merely part of a natural cycle of birth, reproduction and death. Sadly, some nymphs fail even to know the briefest of love affairs, and in this painting death is arriving early. If anyone cares about what happened to the trout, I must record that I gave it back to the water whence it came.

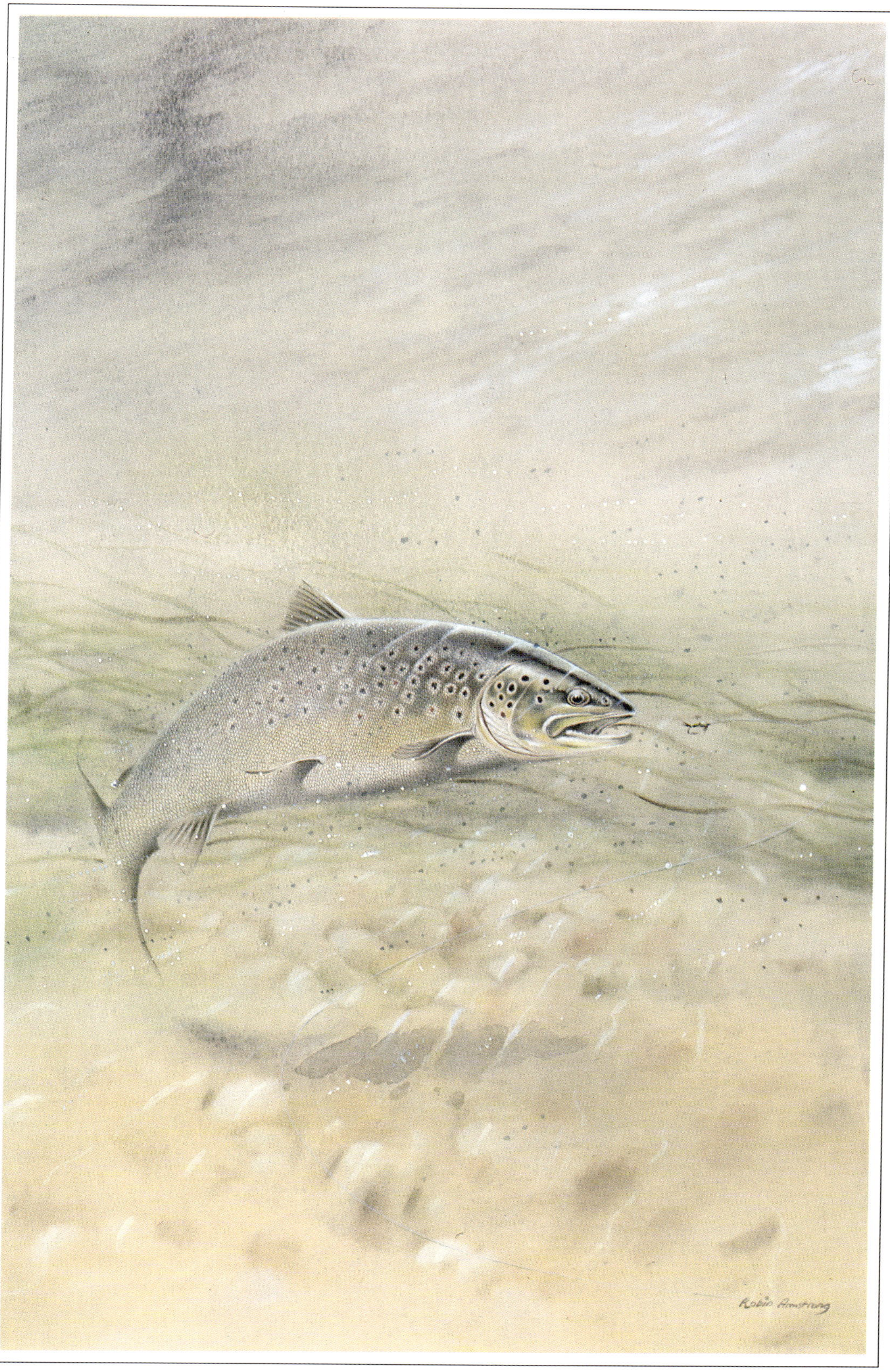
Robin Armstrong

The fisherman who has no respect for his quarry is no fisherman; if trout were easy to take, there would be little point in taking them. If supper is all you are after, you might as well chuck a carbide grenade into the nearest pool. Trout fishing is not for those who measure success in pounds avoirdupois; its satisfactions are more subtle than that. It is a pursuit of artists and heroes, of scholars and practical men, of dreamers and doers, of a diverse company of the great, the good and the very wise. Trout are modestly sized but immeasurably noble fish, and those who fish for them are also out of the common run – rounded and sensible people, but with just a touch, a small and controllable touch, of obsession in them; people who sometimes become mildly eccentric (although rarely mad) but who are always too busy pursuing their passion to have time for any criminal instincts.

And few are dull, as any landlord of a riverside inn will readily confirm, although fly fishing does breed a certain common sense and gravitas. The man who knows the difference between a Red Hackle and a Gold Ribbed Hare's Ear (a fly said to have been known to the Romans), and when to use which, is likely to know much else as well, just as the true craftsman in one trade can usually master others. Even the newcomer to fishing cannot work the banks of a trout stream without acquiring some wisdom, and the old hands constitute some of the sagest men I have ever known.

Do I exaggerate? Perhaps, but not by much. I do think that we who have walked the tumbling burns of Dartmoor, picking our careful way over rocky outcrops or through soaking bog, seeking scarce brownies; we who have, by contrast, idled about one small reach of a chalk stream, trying to remain unseen while tempting one of their wary cousins into an uncharacteristic mistake; we who have watched pools and eddies and observed our prey carefully – we all experience the true joy that comes from studied and hard-earned success. The lucky tyro may catch his first fish with his first cast, but we know that most trout will trouble us more than that. There has never been a trout that can be taken easily; in all their manifestations and widely different habitats, they have always afforded first-class sport. It is little wonder that for a century and more, men have been taking special pains to see that some of these fish should continue to be able to live (if sometimes only to die suddenly) in the smart chalk-stream surroundings which so well befit them.

CHAPTER 3

· Primus inter Pares ·

> Until I made my earliest attempts on this historic Hampshire stream, I was really under the impression that I knew something of dry-fly fishing and fancied myself rather a good hand at it. I was quickly disillusioned: the Houghton trout were not to be beguiled by any of my feeble attempts, and the necessity for devoting myself to a prolonged study of the river, the fish and their habits, and the insects on which they fed, was soon strongly impressed on my mind.
>
> Frederic M. Halford
An Angler's Autobiography

ALL rivers, as Orwell might have said, are equal, but some are more equal than others. And the Hampshire Test, I suggest, is one of these. In any book on chalk streams, only the most curmudgeonly would deny it a chapter to itself. This is a river which has not (yet) been despoiled, blessed not only in its chalky origins, which ensure it a fairly steady supply of clear water, but in the lovely landscape through which it flows. Here, above and below Stockbridge, are fishing places to please trout men from every part of the world, as hallowed to anglers as the Royal and Ancient is to golfers. Even the envious who might be inclined to question the privileged position of those who enjoy its fishing rights can hardly fail to be captivated by it. It steals hearts; it fills the prosaic with poetic thoughts; it makes old men feel young. It is the kind of river that a rich Texan, seeing it for the first time, might want to wrap up and take home with him, ripple by gentle ripple, trout and all, to set down at the bottom of his ranch-house garden along with an old red telephone box.

The Test, in short, is quintessentially English. Few stretches of water offer the same sense of timeless repose; fishing the Test, you become one with a wealth of angling history. Walton almost certainly knew this river. It was here that Marryat and Halford researched the insect life and pondered the wisdom of stocking with stew-reared fish. It was here that the Houghton Club began its august existence. The hut Halford used is still standing; many of his fellow fishers' photographs show views of places which are virtually unchanged since his Victorian heyday, and some of today's meadows still look as though they have been nourishing the same cows since time began.

The river itself begins, modestly enough, somewhere close to grid reference 530500, about ten miles east-north-east of Andover. That, at least, is what the

· Halford's hut ·

A HUT is a hut is a hut, and there is not much more to be said about it, except that this particular hut was used by Halford and still stands as a reminder of him and his many friends. I hope it will survive for ever. To remind myself of his five principles on fishing the dry-fly (fish the single trout, not the water; present an artificial as close to the natural as possible in size and colour; float it with its wings cocked; land it delicately and let it drift without drag; don't let any part of yourself or your rod be seen), I once tried reducing them to doggerel. This, with no pretensions and a warning not to flaunt it among proper verse writers, was the result.

> Do not merely fish the water,
> Find a single feeding trout.
> Then present an artificial
> Like the fly he's wild about.
> Let it float with wings up, cock-ed,
> And with gentle fall alight;
> Drifting dragless and with neither
> Fisherman nor rod in sight.

If anyone ever invents a tape recorder-cum-time machine to bring back conversations past, I should like to hear the best of the discussions which must have taken place in this hut.

Whitchurch

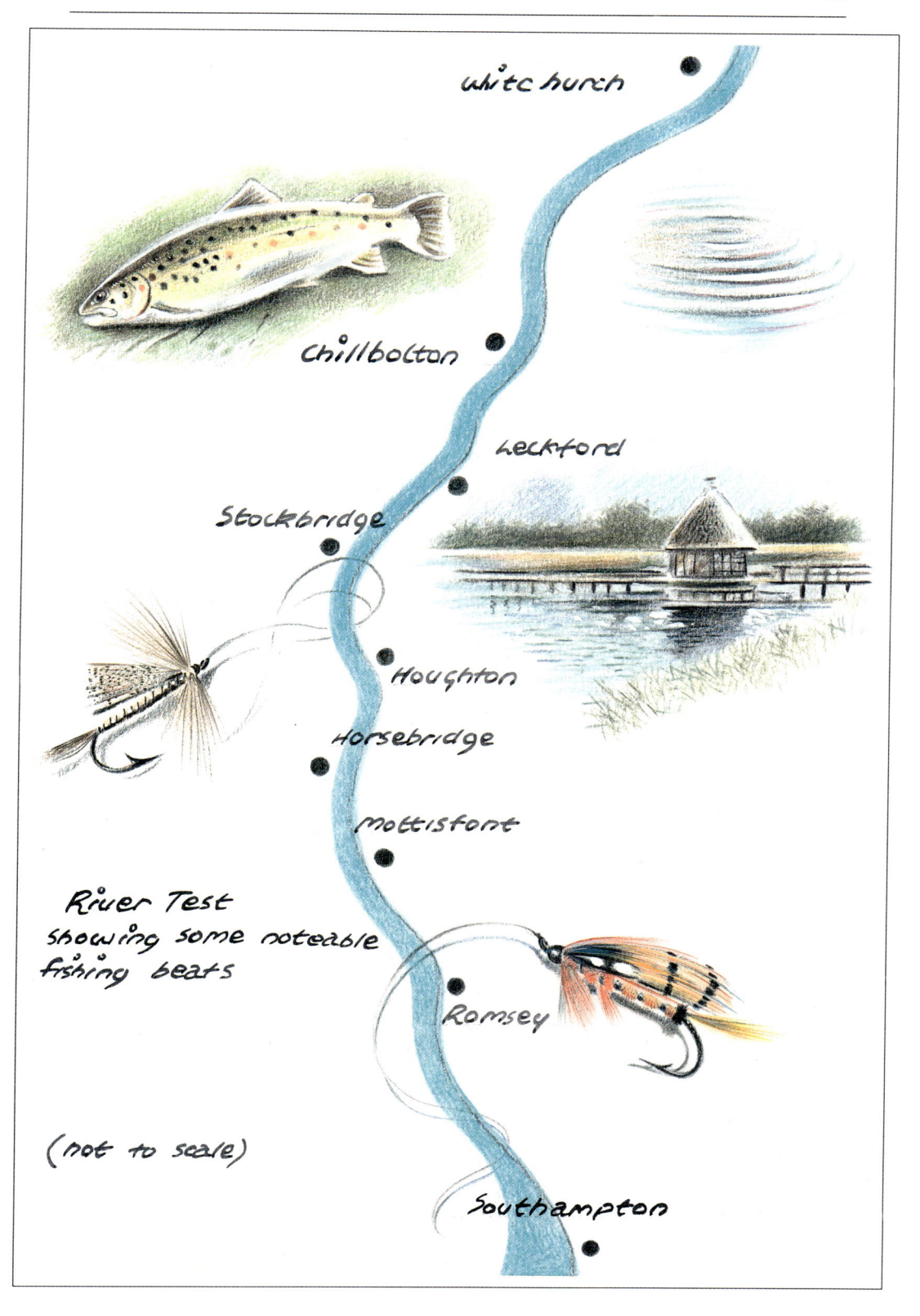

Chillbolton

Leckford

Stockbridge

Houghton

Horsebridge

Mottisfont

River Test
showing some noteable
fishing beats

Romsey

(not to scale)

Southampton

neat lower-case letters of the Ordnance Survey map tell us. But the story is surely less straightforward. Beneath whatever small spring or patch of Hampshire mire from which it is said to flow, might there not be some other more elemental source, many dark miles away through the chalk – some subterranean Elysium, perhaps, where trout waters are specially blended under the benign supervision of the great Walton himself?

The truth, although I should prefer to believe my own fancy, is doubtless as prosaic as the cartographers claim. Yet the cheerful pagans of earlier times might not have found my speculations odd. To them, water was one of the four principal elements (fire, earth and air being the other three), so the gentle and life-giving Test, lazily meandering through the lush Hampshire meadows, must surely have had some place in their pantheon.

Trout fishermen would agree that it is a unique river, with its own magic and character – placid enough, yet far from amenable to neat classification. Even as it grows, it divides and subdivides and reaches off into wayward branches, as if to assert its very English independence. Its final destination, something over forty miles from its beginnings, is the English Channel, but it takes its time getting there, curling round one meadow and creeping back to avoid another. Who can say with certainty which should be defined as its trunk and which its attendant limbs?

The map makers have drawn the Test in flat blue, meticulously following its bends and loops and studiously noting the man-made weirs and sluices which mark its southerly progress. But what they cannot show is the quality of the river, its speed and flow, the colour and composition of its water, the measure of the fish to be found in it, and the senior place it enjoys in the chalk streams' table of precedence. No two-dimensional drawing nor prose description can ever quite capture its character, which can be properly experienced only by those who work it. And they, diversely but unanimously, all seem to agree that the Test does indeed merit singular praise. Generations of anglers since man first invented rod and line have fished it with feelings of unqualified delight. Its water is clear and unpolluted; its fish are sporting and well shaped; and it runs through country which is as archetypally rural English as any could be.

To see it best, perhaps, you need to rise early on a summer morning when the mist, a sure token of warmth to come, wreathes above it in lazy wisps, like those in a Chinese painting. Or on a still evening, 'quiet as a nun, breathless with adoration', just before dark when the traffic has slackened a bit and the midges are out and you can smell freshly mown lawns and hear the occasional tiny plop of a late-rising fish. There are broader and more spectacular vistas in the world, but few can match the sheer tranquillity of this Hampshire riverscape. Even the most Philistine of visitors is touched by the poetry of it all.

In places, the scenery cannot have changed much since Tudor times. The same meadows fill with wild flowers; the same trees, scarcely touched by the gales of

1987's wild October, stand squarely where they always did. And even the sheep, ruminating under the tidy Hampshire sky, look as though they have hardly moved since they were first painted into an eighteenth-century landscape. Surely all but the most competitive angler could fish here for a week and catch nothing, yet still go home well content. Only the modern roads and the noise of traffic and aircraft intrude; mostly, everything is as it always was, down to the names of the farm workers and fish keepers whose families have lived here for generations.

The Test is a river which inspires the most pedestrian of anglers to dream of new Jerusalems. It is set in countryside where prospects only rarely fail to please and where man, for once, has done almost nothing vile. Here you can still find (some) banks where wild thyme grows, where willows have not been grubbed out, nor hedges destroyed, where bees suck greedily at cowslips untainted by pesticides, where meadowsweet and unruly buttercups still flourish in pastures which have not yet been put to the barley-man's powerful plough.

This is the sort of country where you could almost bring yourself to believe, as you did in childhood, that badgers do call on water-rats, and that toads do drive fast cars along the rural by-ways. It is a landscape still belonging to an earlier age, a landscape not yet captured by twentieth-century bad taste. People fishing at Mottisfont could put themselves into any century they wished and not have their fancies disturbed too much.

By happy accident, no big towns have established themselves on the Test, except at its mouth. From Overton in the north (population 4000 give or take a new house or two) to Whitchurch and Longparish, where the river begins to fork, there are no places on its banks, other than Stockbridge and Romsey, large enough to warrant even a single line in the Automobile Association's guide book.

This is a rural river, lazy and timeless. It was made for fly fishing and firm trout. It was made for fine afternoons (and some not so fine) 'on the water', and for friendships cemented afterwards in the local inns or, more grandly, the Grosvenor Hotel in Stockbridge, where the Houghton Club has its privileged headquarters. This is a river that fisherman from all over the world come to fish, drawn by its beauty and the starring role it has played in the history of the dry-fly techniques developed by the Marryat and Halford generation.

The *Haig Guide to Trout Fishing in Britain* sensibly divides the Test into three parts: the upper, from its source to Chilbolton, ranging in depth from 18 inches to roughly 4 feet; the middle, thence to Romsey through Stockbridge and King's Sombourne, where the pools are wider and deeper; and the lower, which merges into the altogether busier and more frenetic Southampton Water.

Broadly, the upper and middle stretches offer the same sport: wild brown trout and a few stocked rainbows, all of them wary and easily spooked by a careless approach or a clumsy cast. The lower reach, where the water is less alkaline, still supports salmon and sea-trout, but runs have declined over the years.

According to the *Guide*, the Test of the 1920s was 'one of the best all round trout and salmon rivers in the country', but its main reputation, jealously preserved by the guardians of its upper waters, is that of a trout river. Halford, in his diaries, writes little about salmon. Even in his day it seems clear that the pursuit of trout was his and his friends' first true love. Salmon was for eating but trout, artfully, scientifically, honourably and doggedly sought, was the fish which most aroused the angler in him, as well as in many others.

In those days, the Test was less threatened than it is now. The building of a new country house close to the river would cause concern over the sewage it might generate; or fishermen might perhaps worry about over-fishing, or stocking policies, or the effects of over-zealous weed cutting. But all these matters now seem of little import when compared with the havoc which can be caused by one careless discharge of farm slurry, or a build-up of nitrates in the water, or the digging of a gravel pit. Today's hazards make yesterday's seem trivial; now, a single thoughtless mistake or uncaring act can ruin a river for months or even years to come.

So far, the Test has escaped the worst of man's ravages. It has not known the horrors heaped upon the industrial rivers of the north and east. As far as we know, its fate in the Middle Ages was to provide sport and food for fat abbots and outrageous nuns; perhaps then, and certainly later, it also supported some profitable mills. But it was never abused as were, say, the Tyne or the Humber. When it came to be notable above the average for followers of the dry-fly, perhaps at the beginning of the last century, it must have been bright and sparkling, more or less as God surely intended it to be. John Waller Hills, in his elegantly written classic *Summer on the Test*, thought its colour in his day (1924) 'not as clear as it was'. But he could still claim – and his authority was better founded than most – that 'in spite of the wear and tear of time, in spite of man and his many iniquities, the essential Test remains to us. She is still the greatest river in the world: and it is to be hoped that this present generation will hand her on unspoilt to their successors.'

To the words of Hills I can only add a fervent 'Amen'. We are two generations on from that to which he refers, and more cognisant, perhaps, of environmental issues. But whether we in turn will be successful in preserving for our children what was preserved for us will be discussed later. For now it is enough to note that the Test is as precious a God-given heritage as we have; were man to despoil it, I doubt if it could ever be reshaped to its present near-perfection.

CHAPTER 4

· *Halford's River* ·

Few serious fly fishers have not heard of Frederic M. Halford. Even in Japan and America (he had a fondness for American rods) he is known and respected as one of the earliest and most literate protagonists of modern dry-fly techniques. The articles (mostly published in *The Field* under the pseudonym 'Detached Badger') and books in which he described his angling theories, outlined his methods and shared his experiences brought him a wide and appreciative audience. Among earnest Victorian and Edwardian fishermen, men who approached their sport with all the gravity proper to their industrious and enquiring age, his reputation stood high.

Halford has been called, not without truth, the father of dry-fly fishing, and since much of his life was spent on the chalk streams, particularly the Test, he more than deserves mention in any contemplation of the rivers to which he devoted so much study. For it was from them that he taught himself about entomology, the mechanics of the river's flow, the management of weeds and much else. He was the kind of enthusiast who applied himself totally to whatever he did, but unlike some, he had an uncommon ability to marry theory with practice. His knowledge of the Test and its attendant streams and carriers was extensive and detailed, and it is as right for his name to be associated with that river as it is for the name of the ecclesiastical naturalist Gilbert White to be forever linked to the village of Selbourne.

Halford was born in 1844 into a comfortable middle-class business family in the English Midlands. Queen Victoria was then seven years into her reign, securely married to the worthy Albert, and on her way to becoming a national institution. Not then as well loved and respected as she later became, she sat on a throne more secure than most, and was much better advised. Within her complacent realm (or at least the affluent parts of it), all appeared well under an English heaven. Over the next seven decades of Halford's life, apart from the Crimea and various small colonial wars fought mainly by a handful of professional soldiers, the country was to enjoy unprecedented domestic peace and a prosperity which, despite many blemishes, made us the envy of the world. Halford, angler and naturalist, entered a warm and secure kingdom in which to pursue his gentle passion.

His childhood was conventional and happy. He was touched by a love for fishing at an age when most of us can barely shape written words, and his first memories were entirely of the delight he took in exploring the small pond near his family home. Under the tutelage of his elder brother and sister, he would try for small roach and perch with a gut hook for hours on end. When the weather forbade outdoor excursions, he would risk his mother's displeasure by fishing with a bent pin for a housemaid's cap from the stairs below the hall. (There is no record of the housemaids' opinion of this.)

Much as future tennis champions, in the absence of a proper court, hit balls against a household wall, Halford seems to have spent many (if not most) of his spare moments perfecting both his knowledge of fish and his casting skills. The family moved to London when he was only seven, but he was more than old enough to continue a determined and single-minded pursuit of the perch and roach which then flourished in the waters of Hyde Park's Serpentine.

In his own words, he was the archetypal 'worm at one end and fool at the other', the butt of fellow schoolboys' pranks. But he clearly cared more for angling than the opinions of his classmates. When offered the choice of a present he would plump for a fishing expedition to the Thames, and when he won a couple of school prizes at the age of thirteen and his father rewarded him with a set of fishing gear, he was delighted. Clearly, he was a boy possessed by one sport, a natural fisherman whose first fine angling rapture developed into a deep and consuming passion.

Halford wrote his own story in *An Angler's Autobiography*, and no work was more aptly titled. It says little about his parents and his wife, his business or finances, his thoughts and feelings on any subject other than that of fishing. He was certainly not a man to bare his soul to public view, nor to drag his family into the limelight. Reading between the lines might convey something of his nature in general, and of his place in the Victorian social order, but nothing of his tastes in particular, nor of his politics. Whether he liked roast beef or brown bread, Charles Dickens or Mrs Henry Wood, is not disclosed. Certainly in those of his books and papers I have seen, his life away from the river is neither explained nor explored.

Halford's obituaries give evidence of his kindness and decency, his enjoyment of life and his intellectual ability. But his own writings shed little light on his private persona. He saw himself, at least publicly, primarily as an exponent of the art of fly fishing, whether wet or dry, and secondly as a naturalist. If ever he thought to be remembered, it would be for his contribution to the sport he followed all his life. All else, in his eyes, would have been an irrelevance. So this, perhaps, is how he should be celebrated – as an angler and innovator, an improver and early conservationist. If he had private warts, they were not apparent. He was a straightforward Victorian gentleman, eminent in his field, relentless in his pursuit of scientific truth, and an earnest and generous communicator of his discoveries.

A hundred years ago the population of England was little more than half what it is now, and, more importantly, there were no motor cars. Halford lived mainly in London, but when he came down to Hampshire the only intruders on his bucolic contentment were likely to be the friends whom he invited to fish with him. He had the leisure and sufficient funds to pursue his idyll. In this he was fortunate, and he relished his good fortune. In the manner of the best of his generation, he resolved to share his own delight in fishing as widely as he could. He believed most strongly in giving back to his chosen sport as much as he took from it, and practised this belief throughout a long fishing life. Every year, like a beneficent squire, Halford would organise a thoroughly English parish meal to which his London friends, fishing neighbours and most of the villagers, together with workers on the river, would be invited. In articles and books he spread his gospel with missionary zeal.

Halford was thoughtful, far-seeing and concerned for the future of the rivers on which he fished. His technical knowledge ran wide and deep, and his practical sense interpreted his theoretical insights. With his expertise in the fields of chalk-stream management, fish stocking, fly tying and fishing methods, few of his equals in one aspect of the art could match him in all. As *The Times* commented in reporting his death, he was probably the most prominent angler of his day, and he was certainly one of the most respected. More than seventy-five years after his death, his writings can still both enlighten us and evoke admiration for his skill, flair and percipience. I can only suggest that his works are worth seeking and reading, since no brief summary of them could capture the uniquely earnest Victorian flavour of a writer dedicated to explaining his discoveries.

Even in that less crowded age, Halford had more leisure than most in which to pursue his obsession. While other Victorians spent their days ruling the Empire, or developing great industries, or consolidating their hold on financial markets, he seemed content, having achieved financial security, to concentrate on fly fishing, a sport which, by 1879 when Halford began keeping his fishing diary, was being taken up by increasing numbers of the newly emerging affluent middle class.

At that time, everything to do with angling was flourishing, and anglers were well served by a wealth of Victorian craftsmen. Tackle makers were thriving; gentlemen's outfitters were doing a fine trade in knickerbockers and Norfolk jackets, and the illustrious Hardy Brothers were steadily working towards the production of my favourite reel, the original of the 'Perfect' series. And with 20 million fewer people on this sceptred isle, those Britons who could afford to fish (even then, a rod on certain 'fashionable' rivers such as the Test was relatively expensive) enjoyed idyllic, uncrowded conditions in which to do so.

Apart from facing fewer pressures on the available river space, the Victorian gentleman must have fished in much the same way as we do, at least superficially. Halford's fishing diaries, conscientiously kept from 1879 until he died in 1914, and then continued by his son until 1929, were lent to me by his great-grandson. They show exactly what he caught, where and with whom, and provide us with a record of the Test (where he mainly fished) which must be unique. I doubt whether,

· *A fishing seat on the Test at Mottisfont* ·

This is hardly a fishing picture but a reminder that rivers are splendid places where one can simply sit and do very little except think and reflect. If poetry takes its origins from emotions recollected in tranquillity, then anyone who sits here might hope to become a poet, for a more tranquil place in which to relive old fishing triumphs it would be hard to find. I liked this arrangement of wood and water. The seat is crude, but right; unlike an artificially rustic bench, produced to order for a supermarket, this is a genuine piece of country woodwork. You can sit on it and muse on times past, times present and times to come without feeling mournful about any of them. Some day, perhaps, when I am very old and very grey and the strength has gone from my casting arm, and I can barely see a trout at ten paces, I will have myself brought here, well wrapped up against the river's chill, simply to dream about happy days and absent friends.

Too many benches, shaped and ordered to some European Community standard and passed as safe by the health inspectors, would ruin our bank-sides. But an occasional resting place such as this one reminds nature that man can sometimes add to her native scenery as well as detract from it.

Brown trout coming to net

outside the royal households (or perhaps the Houghton Club), any similar fishing records spanning such a long period still exist.

It is interesting to speculate about those earlier days. Were the summers balmier? Were catches heavier? Were flies the same as now, or anglers much different from us? Certainly, to answer at least the last question, they were as concerned about pollution as we are. And certainly they seem to have discussed much the same subjects over a pint in the Grosvenor Hotel. But not many present-day fishermen can be more or less retired from business in early middle age, as Halford was, free to devote most of the rest of their lives to such a detailed pursuit of every aspect of the dry-fly art.

From about 1884 onwards, all Halford's spare time was engaged in the study of trout: their breeding and physical characteristics; their eating habits; their taste in flies and the methods employed to catch them. In the season which began in April 1889, he spent seventy-two days on the river, taking eighty-nine trout weighing in total 111 lb 15 oz (slightly over 50 kilogrammes), plus three grayling. All of these were caught on various parts of the Test.

Most of us would not feel displeased with an April in which we went out for nine days and took twelve trout averaging just over a pound each. But this is what Halford did, although not always in halcyon circumstances. Then, as now, the weather in the early part of the fishing season could be inclement and the cold wind unkind. When Browning yearned 'to be in England, now that April's there', he had perhaps forgotten that an English spring can be cold and uncomfortable, even for those with strong blood and warm clothing. Yet if not all of the days in that April of a hundred years ago sparkled in sunshine, Halford still went out; clearly he was not simply a fair-weather fisherman but one who took the rough with the smooth.

Here, then, for I think they are of some interest – if only for the flies he used – are the details of nine not untypical Halford days in that long-ago spring. He was fishing at Kingsworthy in Hampshire, on the limpid Itchen, and the notes are as he wrote them.

6 April: wind north easterly, using a Medium Olive, took one trout of 1 lb 12 ozs. One friend at the lower end of the water took three brace. A fair hatch at 12.30; fish just commencing to rise, then a cold shower and thunder, after which no fly and no rise.

8 April: wind easterly, using a Hare's Ear; Gold Ribbed Hare's Ear, and a Dark Olive Quill, took four trout totalling 4 lbs 13 ozs, and ranging from 13 ozs to 1 lb 12 ozs. Lost three and returned one. A little fly about 11.30 and a few fish rising badly up to 4 p.m. A friend fishing nearby drew blank.

9 April: wind ENE, using a Gold Ribbed Hare's Ear took one of 1 lb 12 ozs. Lost two, while a friend took one. Misty with light rain: fish rising badly and not much fly.

10 April: wind north westerly, using Gold Ribbed Hare's Ear and a Dark Olive Quill took four averaging 1 lb 1 oz. Returned one. Not much fly and very little rise. Only fished until 2.30.

25 April: wind north easterly, using Gold Ribbed Hare's Ear. Caught nothing and returned one. Wind very strong with occasional sun. Not much fly. Louis Montague [presumably a friend] with Lock [a famous keeper] caught one of 1 lb 7 ozs.

26 April: wind southerly, again using the Gold Ribbed Hare's Ear, took one of 1 lb 14 ozs. Montague, again with Lock, rolled over four and lost two. A fine morning, clouding over later with rain in the afternoon, and fish jumping.

27 April: wind southerly, using a Pale Olive Dun, took one trout of exactly 1 lb and another of 11 ozs. Returned and turned over several. A little fly, but not many rising. Fishing all over by 2.30.

29 April: wind southerly. Did not fish except over three and hooked one of them. Yarned with Cary [?] and turned 10,000 fry into pond.

30 April: wind south easterly. Caught nothing. Fish rose well about 1 to 1.30. Very heavy rain and one clap of thunder, then a little fly after this but no rise. G.S.M. at upper end of water broke fly in one fish and only saw one other rise.

These are only a few days from one year of Halford's fishing life, chosen simply because exactly a hundred years had passed since they were recorded. The diaries reveal no startling trends. Over the years the average weight of the trout caught does not vary greatly, nor do the average numbers caught per fishing day. Taking each of the five decades beginning in 1879 and ending in 1929, the average weights of all his and his son's catches (to the nearest ounce) were 1 lb 9 oz, 1 lb 6 oz, 1 lb 10 oz, 1 lb 11 oz and 1 lb 12 oz: a marginal increase over the years perhaps, but one that only a very brave statistician would regard as significant.

Plus ça change, the more fishing stays the same. I have not had the chance to fish the Test in April, so I am not sure how Halford's experience would compare with that of today's fisherman working the same stretch of water. One day, if I can find a host kind enough, I should like to follow his long-gone footsteps and see what happens on the same days of the year in the same locations. For the places he fished have changed less than many. His bankside hut at Mitchingham still looks out on to the same placid stream on which he spent so much time.

I suspect that not many of today's anglers – even those rich enough to fish the Test – are able to spend four to eight hours on the river almost every day throughout the fishing season, which is what Halford's diary shows him to have done in 1888. Nowadays, earning and spending money take up too many hours for any of us to dedicate our time as he did. But at least he employed his fishing hours seriously, studying the entomology of the river and making careful note of his successes and failures. And he wasn't always killing fish. Long before the good

· *Grayling feeding between reed beds* ·
· *Head study of a grayling* ·

'WHAT is the artist doing,' asks the purist, 'to waste his time painting pictures of fish like these?' I have to answer that I am painting grayling, and to blazes with the purists. Like other members of the Grayling Society, which is still very active, I am not one to neglect this underrated fish. Inferior to the trout as it may be, both in the sport it offers and in its flavour, the grayling is a handsome and firm-bodied fish, well deserving of the artist's attentions. Under the grey skin of one freshly caught, it is fleetingly clothed in all the colours of the rainbow. I can't remember precisely where I completed these studies, except that they came from Hampshire where, over the years, I have seen and caught more grayling than I have in Devon.

Grayling have long been feared by fishery owners who claim that they bully trout, steal the trouts' food and generally behave like ill-bred louts. I suspect that this is too black a picture, but then, I am not a fishery owner. I do admit that an individual grayling can be a nuisance when it steams up from the bottom to grab the fly meant for a trout, and I can understand why many anglers regard them as a pest. But are not some of their failings compensated for by the fact that one can fish for them in winter when trout and salmon become forbidden fruit? Even if they fight less well than a healthy trout, it is better to have fly fishing of a sort rather than no fly fishing at all.

Known in the north as 'umber' and in official circles as 'thymallus' because they are said to smell of thyme when freshly caught (although I have not sensed this), grayling make good eating provided they are carefully headed and cleaned, with scales and fins removed. The flesh in winter is firm and delicately flavoured, with a taste (according to a remark by Charles Cotton in *The Compleat Angler*) 'little inferior to the best trout'. I am not sure that I would go quite that far, but nor would I refuse grayling if the menu lacked fresh sea-bass or salmon.

Grayling lie very low in the water, rising almost vertically from the depths to snatch at a fly and then diving down again, all in one swift movement. Perhaps because they come up from the bottom, the refraction which distorts perception must affect them as it affects humans, since, unlike the average trout, they often miss their target fly.

From the time people began to record such things, grayling have always been found on the Test, and nineteenth-century trout men removed them by the hundreds. Even in recent decades they have been found in great numbers. Mick Lunn, the famous Houghton keeper, is reported as saying that he had 'buried so many grayling [netted or electro-fished from the Test] in his garden' that he needs 'a pair of steps to pick his Brussels sprouts'.

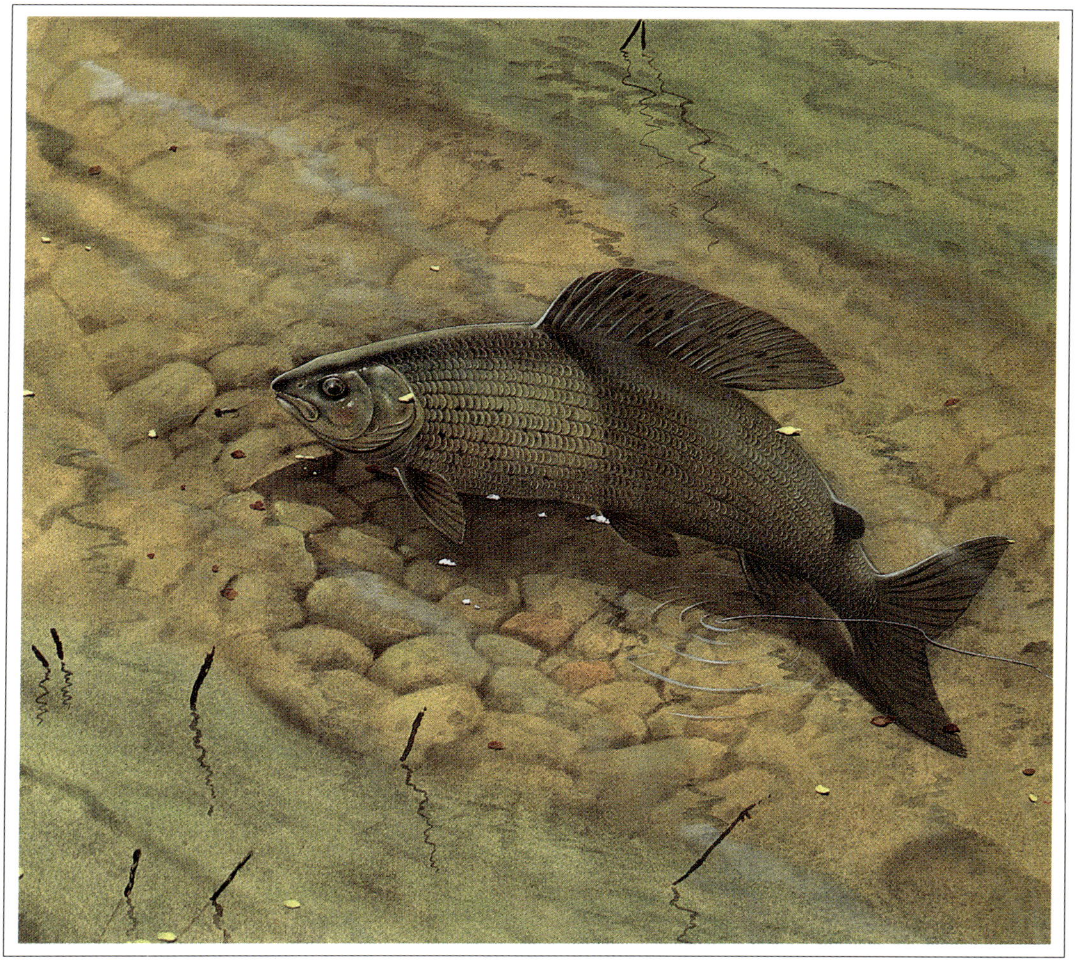

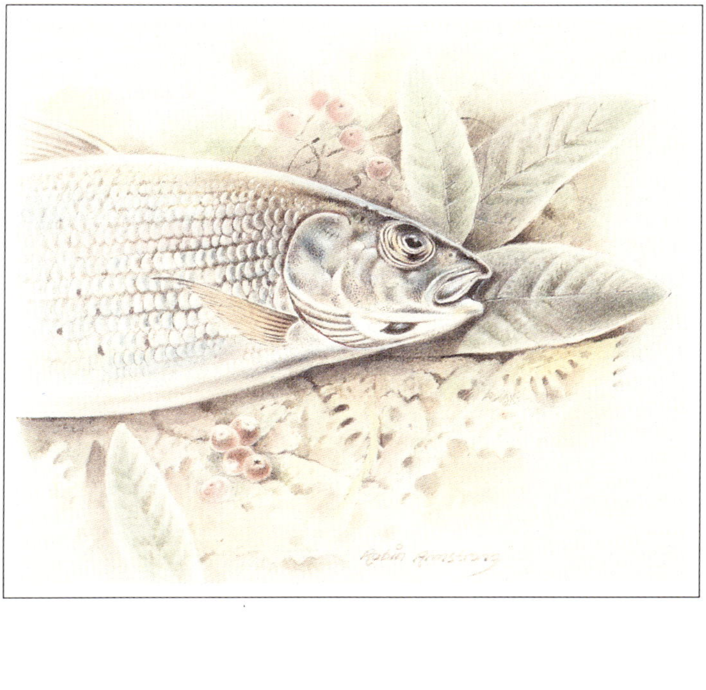

men and true from Colorado began to think of 'catch and release', Halford was throwing fish back. In an era when some of his compatriots, including royalty, would think nothing of taking five or six dozen salmon a day from a Scottish loch or a Norwegian fiord and, lacking the facilities to freeze them, leaving them to waste, Halford was quietly extolling the merits of, and himself following, a less murderous approach. If the term 'conservationist' had then been current, that appellation would have fitted him very well, since he was keenly aware of the need for a long-term approach to river management and always anxious to pass on the river in a better state than he found it.

Halford took nothing for granted. To quote an encomium in the *Journal of the Fly Fishers' Club* for the spring of 1914, he was always 'thorough', building up his experience brick by brick with no short cuts. When he first took 'trout fever' it was on the Wandle, 'a beautiful stream with a good store of singularly handsome "fario", and a regular company of gentlemen fly-fishers' but not many dry-fly men. It was probably amid this company that he first became fascinated by the dry-fly method, to the theory of which, from about his early thirties onward, he then devoted so much of the rest of his fishing life.

One claim he never made, although some of the older dry-fly school might have hoped otherwise, was that this was the only way to fish. He remained faithful to the dry-fly only so long as it was producing results: if it ceased to do this, and if conditions favoured the wet-fly, he had no inhibitions about switching. To him, the dry-fly versus wet-fly debate was simply a technical question, not to be clouded by undertones of sporting snobbery and arguments about what is and what is not good fishing form. But that is another subject in itself, to be contemplated in a separate chapter. For now, let us leave the shade of Halford undisturbed by controversy, for whatever is thought of his approach to trout fishing, there seems little doubt (from reading both what he wrote himself and what others wrote about him) that he was very much a gentleman.

CHAPTER 5

· *The Quadrilateral* ·

IN March 1893 Messrs F.M. Halford, N. Lloyd, B. Field and W.Q. Orchardson R.A., leased Ramsbury Fishery on the Kennet from Sir Francis Burdett for seven, fourteen or twenty-one years at the lessees' option. Halford, advised by his good friend and mentor G.S. Marryat, appears to have been the principal instigator of this arrangement, but all four shared equally in the costs. Judging from their London addresses, Halford's co-lessees, like himself, were all men of some substance. When they surrendered the lease, by arrangement, on 30 September 1896, it was because they were dissatisfied with the quality of the fishing, not because of the expense.

The good old days were very good for those blessed with a substantial income. For a price which probably averaged out at under £800 a year between them, the four sporting friends, calling themselves 'The Quadrilateral' (they preferred this description to 'Syndicate', which 'those among us who had business experience . . . too often found synonymous with "Swindle"'), appeared to have acquired five miles of fishing, a roomy old mill house to use as a fishing box, two keepers' cottages and the services of a housekeeper, two river keepers and sundry helpers.

The fishing was in three lengths: two miles on either bank of spawning shallows; one mile of stream running parallel to the main river, on one bank only; and a further two miles of 'sluggish, deep and sometimes muddy' water moving through a series of mill ponds. The Quadrilateral also had the use of the tributaries and carriers attendant upon the main stream.

How the amount they paid for all this would equate with present-day prices is hard to say, since trying to assess the relative value of the pound with any accuracy over such a long period is virtually impossible. But some idea of relative costs, taken from 1884 when the weed growth was luxuriant and The Quadrilateral needed to kill more of that 'destructive bird, the kingfisher', can be gained from the 18 shillings (90 pence) a week dispensed as wages to the newly appointed assistant keeper employed to deal with the extra work.

Are the details of such a friendly enterprise still of interest? I can only record them and let the reader judge for himself. I think they are, since we can see from them how seriously our Victorian predecessors took their fishing, and how much they were prepared to spend to sustain their interest.

Halford's papers include the expenses for only the first two years of the fishery's operation. At the beginning, each of the four participants put in some £1200 in capital, which they topped up the following year. In detail, their expenditure is shown in Table 3, but particular items stand out, such as the keepers' wages at £80 10s in the first year and £107 in the second, and the amounts paid for 'stocking'.

What Halford got out of this (and presumably his fellows enjoyed similar sport) were 126 fishing days over four seasons, with a total catch of 271 trout, each averaging 1 lb 8 oz. What he and his fellows put into it, apart from money, was the work involved in catching over 3000 each of pike and dace, and stocking over 6000 yearling, mainly with Guildford and High Wycombe strains of trout which, according to Halford, would rise better to the small flies than what he described as the 'degenerated Kennet trout'.

And there, fuming if you are a Kennet man, you can leave the matter for the next two statistical pages. Some people can just about tolerate figures; others (I suspect a majority) hate them. But fishing figures are perhaps different, so just for the record let me risk illustrating this gentle excursion into a friendly Victorian angling 'association' with the details below. If Halford's diaries are accurate – and they almost certainly were – his use of Ramsbury was as follows.

Table 1

Year	Fishing days	Fish caught	Total weight	Average weight
1893	52	104	160 lb 6 oz	1 lb 8 oz
1894	32	60	93 lb 11 oz	1 lb 9 oz
1895	27	60	87 lb 13 oz	1 lb 7½ oz
1896	15	47	65 lb 15 oz	1 lb 6½ oz

The detailed numbers killed and stocked, also compiled from the figures in the diaries, indicate some considerable slaughter of pike in The Quadrilateral's first year. By 1896, presumably, even the fiercest of pike must have kept well away from these very unquiet reaches.

Table 2

	Killed			Stocking & Removing		
Year	Pike	Dace	Dabchick	Trout	Trout yearling	Grayling
1893	2087	1141	31	676	2790	322
1894	836	1501	–	4004	1464	25
1895	211	759	–	2428	1976	34
1896	?	?	?	877	–	–

Finally, how was the money spent? This, shown to the nearest shilling (although in the original it was accounted for to the penny), gives the detail for the first two years.

Table 3

	1893 £	1893 s	1894 £	1894 s
Initial expenditure				
Legal costs	26	4		
Repairs to house & stew	280	3		
Furnishings etc	307	10		
Keeper's removal	18	18		
Tools & nets	40	00		
	672	15	134	7
Ordinary expenditure				
Rent	150	00	300	0
Keepers' wages etc	80	9	107	4
Housekeeper's wages etc	17	0	32	0
House expenses	25	1	70	15
Weed cutting & racking	52	17	66	15
Netting	33	16	33	14
Stocking	85	7	35	14
Keepers' clothing	10	16	11	11
Dinner to watchers	4	3	–	–
Cash to watchers	3	0	3	0
Sundries	15	19	34	16
	479	9	696	5
	1152	4	830	12

There is charm, I think, in this meticulous accounting of small sums and the handwritten recording of the detailed supervision these four Victorian gentlemen exercised over their sporting investment. In the report of the year 1894 they noted that the keepers' wage bill came to £107 instead of the £104 in their estimates, when the senior man was given an increase of £3 a year. But they saved a pound on the sum set aside for his water-boots and jacket, which presumably reconciled them to the totally unexpected £2 they had had to spend on 'removing mud'. This was a job which got an accounting line all to itself, and that it was listed separately surely betokens a very proper and wholly admirable regard for the smallest niceties of communal enterprise.

They were serious men in those days: careful, even frugal perhaps, but certainly, at least in Halford's case, fair. They also applied themselves to what they were doing. It would be hard to imagine them leaving everything to the keeper; the 'carry on, sergeant major' approach would have been alien to them. They wanted to know everything that happened, checking the stocking down to the last small trout, noting the precise numbers of pike and dace killed and removed, very smartly recognising the need to give the fish in the stew a more liberal supply of food than in previous years, and carefully recording their appreciation of the services of Mr T. Skelton, their keeper, 'for the satisfactory manner in which his duties [were] performed during the past season'. In short, there was little connected with the fishery in which they did not take an interest. One certainly cannot imagine them simply arriving to fish without regard to what was being done to the waters in which they fished. In modern jargon, they were 'hands-on' managers who recognised that chalk streams, left to themselves, will not produce the finest sport without proper attention to stocks, weeding and careful supervision.

Despite their efforts, however, The Quadrilateral somewhat reluctantly came to the conclusion that the Ramsbury Fishery was not giving good value for money. 'We had fished the water for four consecutive springs and summers and excepting during the mayfly, or quite late in the summer evenings, we had never seen a really good rise of trout such as were so frequent on other chalk streams,' wrote Halford in his autobiography. And despite all they had done to remove the pike, increase stocks and control the weed, their improvements were not producing results, although they took some credit on leaving for filling every yard of the river with trout of strains 'far superior to the indigenous, slimy yellow salmo fario of the Kennet'. And before any Kennet men complain, the quotation marks should be noted: Halford wrote that, not I.

The Quadrilateral, having left their fishery in a better state (and capable of earning a higher rent) than when they found it, broke up in September 1896. Could the four friends who composed it be taken as representative chalk-stream men of their day? Reading of their earnest endeavours at improvement, I suspect they probably could. The Victorians knew that all worthwhile activity demands effort; even leisure was not to be taken without some thought. If some of them elsewhere were ruining northern rivers with their factories, we are lucky that those who fished the Hampshire streams had a better understanding of nature's needs, and cared deeply about the future. Or was it, more simply, just that industry flourished in the Midlands and the North rather more than it did in the South? Whatever the reason, yesterday's men did well to pass on these rivers in good condition, and we should ponder their example as we contemplate the pressing conservation problems of today.

CHAPTER 6

· The Kimbridge Beat ·

Thursday 15 June 1989 was like a day stolen from an earlier age, when meadows were filled with buttercups and old-fashioned roses scented the summer air, when well-mannered gentlemen in white flannels walked ladies with parasols across velvet lawns, and Hampshire was still many a steam-railway mile away from the rat race of London. It was the kind of innocent day which was supposed to have disappeared for ever in the holocaust of the Great War – a day as beautiful as only an English day can be: not over-hot, but sunny and still and shimmering, filled with the droning of a myriad insects and the gentle sounds of river birds voicing their delight in the feast of insects presented to them by the weed cutting.

The very idea of weed cutting was itself evocative of a different time. Nowadays, weeds are often eradicated with chemical sprays and lingering pesticides, and cutting seems old-fashioned and laboured. I thought of Thomas Hardy characters in collarless shirts and open waistcoats – slow, deliberate men rhythmically scytheing their way down river, missing nothing in their timeless progress, pausing for cider perhaps, and good bread and cheese, and mopping the sweat from their honest brows with huge spotted handkerchiefs. I could even see the great F.M. Halford (who took such cutting very seriously) walking the bank in his Norfolk jacket and tie, fussing over the men and supervising their vital work, anxious to make sure that nothing was badly done or overlooked.

But sentiment had not brought me here, although I confess that some nostalgia after reading Halford's fishing diaries could hardly be avoided. I had come to fish the Test, specifically the Kimbridge beat owned by the Orvis Company, who had kindly given me the temporary freedom of their enviable domain. The water was

· Moorhens ·

THESE birds are perhaps the commonest of our water-fowl, but 'commonest' only in a statistical sense since they are far from common in appearance. 'Moorhen' is really a misnomer because they never go near moors, and many bird lovers prefer to call them water-hens. The name is probably a corruption of its original 'mere-hen', a creature of marsh and lake which breeds near fresh water in thick cover. It is not big – about 13 inches is the average length – but it defends its territory very fiercely when necessary. Sometimes it avoids trouble by sinking below the surface like a submarine, leaving its bill sticking up into the air to act as a snorkel. Town dwellers may often see this bird on sewage farms or park lakes.

Birds, like fish, are infinite in their variety. As you become familiar with them you gradually begin to realise that no two are exactly alike, and that even the same birds take on new aspects in changing light. The blue of an air-mail letter remains the same sheet after sheet, but the blue sheen on a moorhen has to be recaptured afresh each time I paint one. If this were not so, wildlife artists might soon become bored; as it is, there are subtle differences of colour tone in every bird or fish we paint, and trying to capture these differences on paper or canvas remains the ambition of most of us for most of our lives.

thick with weed and the trout, in consequence, somewhat disorientated, but I still foresaw no problem in taking them. I sensed plenty of good fish, and tackled up with a light heart. For my rod I chose a 9 foot 3 inch Orvis Spring Creek, with Number 4/5 line – heavy enough, I thought, for the windless conditions. For reel I settled for my favourite Hardy featherweight, making what I smugly decided was a very nicely balanced outfit for my first day of the year on this fine river. I looked forward to what was to come.

Within five minutes I had played, hooked and landed a beautiful ¾ lb grayling: a lovely fish in perfect condition, which almost fell on to my line. It was only one of several which were feeding all over the river, and I more or less resigned myself to grayling for the rest of the day, since few trout seemed to be moving. But my judgement was premature: my next fish was indeed a brownie of about 2 lb, which took my little Green Olive without hesitation. Within ten minutes of getting on to the river, in bright conditions, I had caught two excellent fish.

The Kimbridge beat is almost worth walking for its own sake, although the fish are such that a true angler, finding himself without a rod, would find it hard to resist fashioning himself makeshift tackle from a hazel twig and an unravelled pullover. On this day the weed was coming down-river thick and fast, and the fishing looked to be easy. I decided I would walk to the end of the beat and then change flies and fish on my way back upstream. But as soon as I made the resolution I broke it, seduced by a lovely gentle sucking and rising brown trout. Taking it was too easy. Either I was the most brilliant of fishermen (which I liked to think, as we all do, was just possible), or the fish were intent on cooperating in their own early capture. Perhaps they were humouring me, sensing that I was committed to putting them all back. Whatever the case, I was returning my third catch to the river before I had decided what my afternoon's strategy ought to be.

My surroundings were idyllic. The meadows were alive with common blue butterflies, fluttering and dancing without benefit of breeze, drunken with sunshine and darting above the lush green grass like mobile kaleidoscopes. Grey wagtails, belying the drab adjective, flitted over the stream in great swoops of bright yellow. Moorhens, perhaps the commonest of British water-fowl, cackled and croaked as if on some avian protest march, while dabchicks, more serene and seemingly happier in the water than in the air, swam confidently in and out of the floating weed. The only bird I missed from my Devon rivers was the dipper, which goes one better than the dabchick by actually walking on the bottom of the stream as well as cruising its surface. On that small stretch of river, free for anyone's easy enjoyment, there was a feast of wildlife rich enough for the most demanding of naturalists and country lovers.

There were also many of every sort of fly, particularly the dark blue and dark green damsels. Who, apart from entomologists, knows the difference between these and dragonflies? And who has eyes sharp enough to detect the difference when they are in supercharged flight? Both are members of the order Odonata, a large clan boasting over five thousand species and a common love of the water. Why the Creator needed such diversity in this small line, we shall never know; sufficient that, according to my reference books, dragonflies are bigger than damsels and have front wings bigger than those at the back, while the latter, more delicate, have front and rear wings of equal size.

I admit to being distracted by the wildlife other than the fish, but in this I doubt if I were acting differently from the fathers of modern angling. For they, too, were interested in the river life as well as the chase, and it pleased me to think that I was probably watching the same sorts of birds as my nineteenth-century predecessors. Even if those stout Victorians might have been more than a little upset by the extraneous sounds of helicopters and distant lorries, I doubt if the essential nature of the chalk streams themselves has changed much over the years.

On the way downstream I saw one big trout moving around under a tree, but it was not feeding. Perhaps it was upset at its eviction from a safe place in the weed beds. The cutting disturbs everything. The fishes' normal feeding stations are disrupted, forcing them to move about looking for new places, and it takes at least a fortnight for them to settle down again. But fish are there, and it takes only patience to find them.

I work today in the same way as early fly men might have done, using a little Dark Olive, which I keep oiled, rather than any more modern attraction. Now I'm fishing for a small grayling which I let run for a minute before taking it seriously, only to find it is not a grayling but a big brown trout of some 3 lb in weight and with a handsome appearance. This will be my fourth fish in less than an hour, and after I've persuaded it out of a reed bed I shall need the net to take it. It turns out to be a magnificent specimen, and I put it back with much reluctance, only because I am committed to doing so.

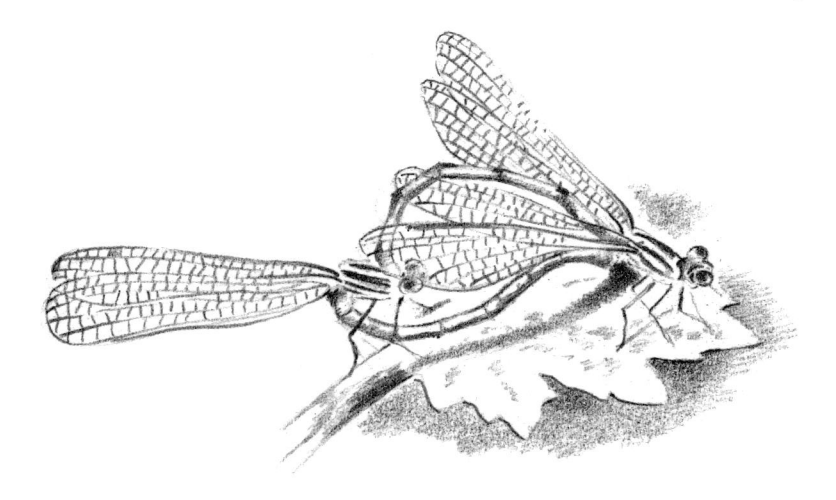

No matter. Just to be here is pleasant enough, even if the feeding seems to have slackened off and all natural activity has apparently ceased. It has not, of course. This is merely a minor lull in the almost constant summer-day sounds of the English countryside. The insects will soon start up again; even the sheep, stretched out in the opposite field like corpses after a battle, may decide they need to stretch their legs and inspect their offspring. It is now exactly four o'clock – time for an early English tea – but the fish are not snatching much at their own afternoon repast in the form of a wealth of insect life. Moving upstream, I am having to pick and choose areas not clogged by weed, forming little dams which will be hard to clear without a rise in the water level. We could do with some rain – preferably at night when it can do its good work without putting us to inconvenience.

Now I have reached a place where two carriers branch off the main channel, and tall reeds make fishing difficult. There must be a nest somewhere in there, as a drab little sedge warbler tries to harass me away from its young. But it fusses to no purpose; I am already committed to walking back upstream from the sluice-gate which marks the end of the beat, and my mind is now on another fish, not the bird-song.

The weed keeps coming down in rafts. Among it is the bloated body of a dead lamb, poignant symbol of all mortality. Other than this sight, my eye rests on nothing but beauty. It seems beyond belief that this precious valley should be even remotely under threat from further water extraction. Already one can see areas of old water meadows which are now dried-out fields. Perhaps the unfriendly roar of the main-line diesel, tearing along from Salisbury to Southampton at 90 m.p.h., is an inevitable consequence of progress, but surely the despoliation of rare meadows is not. There is little enough beauty in city lives to put at risk those places where urban dwellers can come to escape. Here, for example, is a mallard family, sedately swimming in line astern across the main stream, the children looking like models of Victorian propriety as they dutifully coast along in the course set for them by a mother who hardly needs to look around to know that they will faithfully follow where she leads. Do we really want to lose all that? This same family, living on some post-industrial artificial lake, fed twice daily by a 'caring council' and open to public view from 9 until 6, would hardly afford the same joy as they do now.

In this verdant place, everything teems with natural life. Long strands of reed weave in and out, like moving trout. A great bank of light blue speedwell patterns the water above which it spreads in wild but graceful profusion. I cannot see any fish because the water, stirred by the weed cutters further up, is less than clear. Right at my feet a water vole scurries out of the bank and swims to the opposite side. A male, looking for the family's evening meal? A female, off to visit her old mother? It is hard to resist the temptation to ascribe human feelings to creatures which look as though they share our worries and concerns; anthropomorphism was ever an English failing, and I am not immune to it. Meanwhile, the birds continue to feast on all the insects disturbed by the weed cutting. Moorhens, wagtails and here and there a kingfisher vie with each other for places at the rich table, walking along the banks of weed and diving under whenever they see some especially tasty delicacy.

But it was fish that I came for, and at last I can see another one, the first for about half an hour. It is out of reach of all but the most powerful caster, some fifty yards across to the other bank, and my 9 footer rod would hardly take me that distance. As always, the biggest and brightest are inevitably too far away or too deeply entrenched under some impossible overhang, and I shall have to let this one go, keeping it in my mind's eye only to dream about. This is where my close-focus binoculars might have been useful, but I rarely carry them nowadays except when I am specifically going out to watch fish. Nineteenth-century photographs show that many of Halford's friends always took glasses with them. For a long time I mocked the practice, but it can make sense. Even when a fish is only 15 yards away, you can see it in far greater detail through binoculars than with the naked eye. And I should like to have studied this one, disporting safely out of my reach as though it knew my casting limitations. But it makes a fitting end to a wonderful afternoon, since to leave the feast while still slightly hungry is better than to leave feeling over-full. Like General MacArthur, I shall return.

· Salmon leaping after being hooked at Broadlands ·

BROADLANDS Estate lies on the Test just below Romsey, and an excellent short account of its development as a salmon fishery from the 1880s to the present day is given in Charles Bingham's *The River Test*. This painting may be too strong for some squeamish tastes, but hooking fish is the essence of fishing, and this is what salmon usually do before we can successfully land them, or in this case unsuccessfully lose them.

This fish wasn't mine but that of someone who had never before found himself into a twenty-pound salmon and was therefore somewhat awed by the experience. I was merely sketching in the area when I saw him fight this battle, and only later spoke with him to share his disappointment. As with sea-trout, salmon of this size are said to be rarer than they were of old but I cannot produce the statistics to confirm this. Perhaps, like summers of yesterday, the past takes on a rosy glow that the figures often fail to substantiate. In the case of salmon runs, however, the folk tales are almost certainly, and sadly, right. Most of the people to whom I have talked tell me that numbers have declined and are still declining.

'Catching and releasing' trout is something most of us can do without too much heart searching. But returning a big salmon requires a much sterner will. Some day, though, we may all have to learn the discipline necessary to do this.

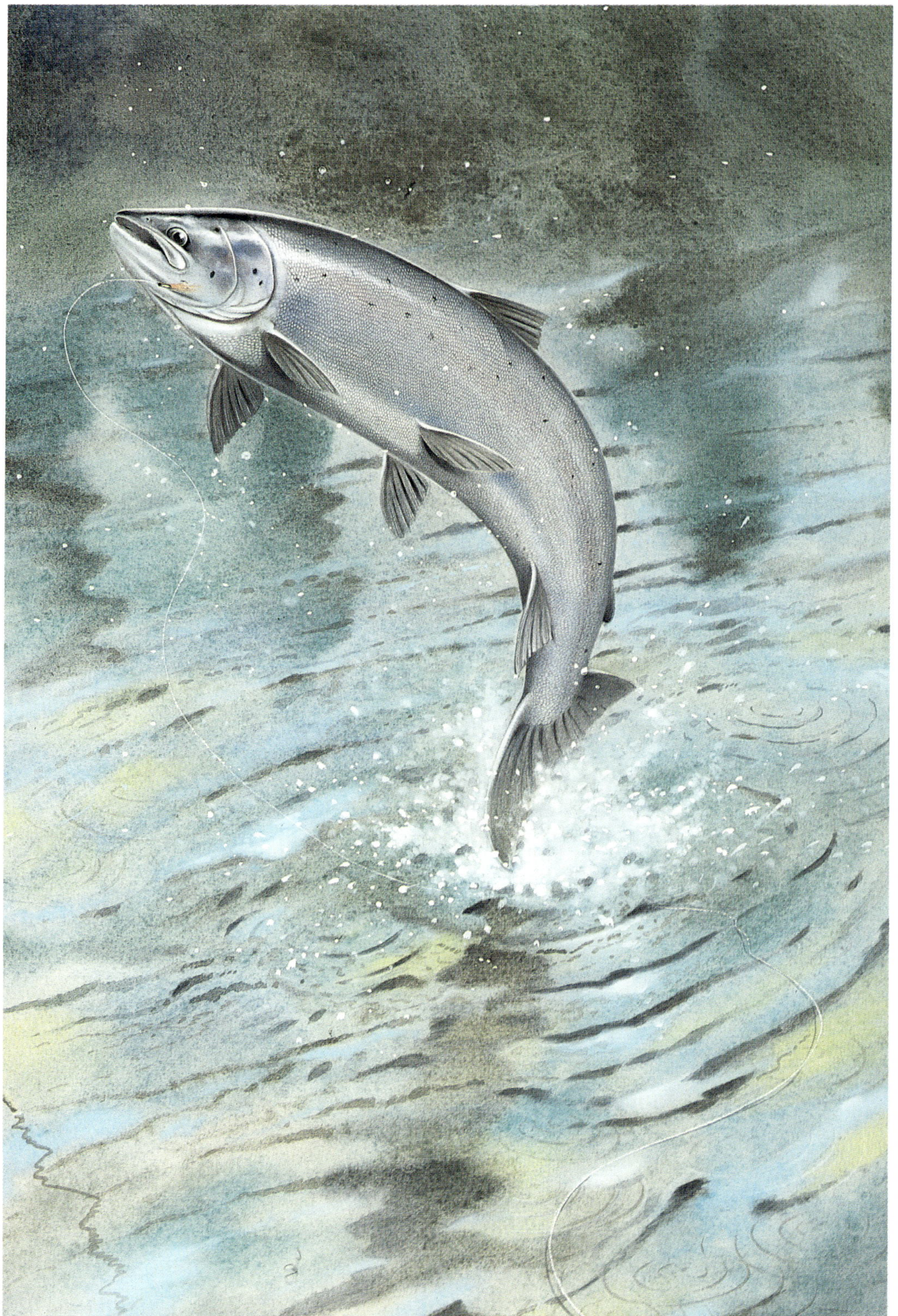
Robin Armstrong '87

CHAPTER 7

· The Upper Avon ·

Let me begin my account of a day on the upper Avon with a momentary diversion to Oxford, where the river is more famous for punts and skinny dipping than for fish. Here is a small city with a wealth of history crowded into the colleges and churches at its hub. Walk south, for example, from the Bodleian Library past the Radcliffe Camera and there, within a few yards, is All Souls College, quietly slumbering in the peace of its 551st year. No undergraduates disturb the calm of its lovely quad, none but the great and the good grace its high table, and only the most illustrious of each generation are elected to its fellowships. Among its distinguished members are the wise and worthy of every sort; it is academe *par excellence*, but academe tempered by the insights and experience of those who work in high places outside its hallowed walls.

Sadly the place is blemished, for no one has proposed Dermot Wilson – a starred first among anglers and a man whose fishing erudition blazes out from a myriad of books and articles, and whose riverine genius enlightens and entertains us all – for election to one of its fellowships. With fishing an art and science as old as time, which must surely rank equal with classics and quantum physics in the order of things, it seems an unhappy oversight much in need of early correction.

Meanwhile, I take simple pleasure in being with him at Heale House on the upper Avon. The day, Friday 16 June 1989, is of another age: hot and sunny, windless and worry free. The weed is not cut, the river is low and clear, and life is perfect. The only small irritation (not difficult to endure because it is a cheerful one) is an accompanying television crew from Harlech Television who seem to expect that a large trout can be caught to order whenever the producer requires it.

Dermot is euphoric. The river suits him: it is languid and less turbulent than the stretch of the Kennet I worked yesterday and it demands more thought from those who fish it. Even if the somewhat over-ebullient television people, rushing about like schoolboys after early prep, make catching fish difficult, they cannot dampen our delight at being here on such a stretch of river and on such a day.

I envy Dermot's Thomas and Thomas 8½ foot cane trout rod, made especially for him and presented to him by those distinguished manufacturers when he was an honorary member of the New York Fly-fishers' Club. His reel is equally splendid and enviable: a Stan Bogdan hand-made specimen which might have cost anything between £500 and £700 if it, too, had not been given to him. Who could fail to catch fish with such equipment – or, in failing, not derive delight from using, however unsuccessfully, something so perfectly crafted?

· *Dabchicks, 'one up, one down'* ·
(overleaf)

THE dabchick, also known more prosaically as the little grebe, is the smallest of our freshwater fowl. I painted these at Bossington, somewhere close to where Wallop Brook joins the Test between the Houghton waters and Mottisfont. The fishing here is said to be as good as I thought it looked, and the dabchicks on this fine morning were like diners discovering a new gourmet restaurant before the crowd arrived to ruin it. I know these birds too well to misread these signs as being indicative of rising trout, but plenty of inexperienced anglers have been known to make that mistake.

This Bossington reach is owned by an estate which takes care of its heritage. Upstream I believe some water-meadows have been lost to crops; ploughing reaches almost to the water's edge, and where silt once settled in the meadows it now runs off into the river. Where grass once grew, cereals have taken over. I am told that in some countries all rivers are bordered by a chain's width of riparian reserve which remains the property of the state. Would this, I wonder, be too radical an arrangement to introduce into England, where riverbank rights have been in private ownership at least as far back as my own historical knowledge extends?

Whether it would or would not, no change in tenure would make much difference to the disporting of my dabchicks, which regard the water as their own, swimming and diving freely and fluently, mostly in search of food but sometimes (I sentimentally suspect) just for sheer joy or to show off their aquatic resourcefulness and versatility. If, like many water birds, dabchicks patter and lumber and chunter and stagger when they take to the air, and are understandably but distinctly awkward and ungainly on land, they are certainly most attractive and at home in water, and fascinating to watch.

I rarely see dabchicks in West Devon since they usually avoid our fast-flowing rivers in favour of slower-moving chalk streams. One also sees them occasionally on lakes and trout fisheries feeding on sticklebacks, insects and so on, but they look best against the kind of background in which I found them here. I painted these two 'one up and one down' because this is a typical pattern, busily seeking food without losing any of their natural elegance.

These birds adopt a courtship ritual which is curious but perhaps very sensible given the mistakes which can be made in these matters. Male and female birds face each other in the water as though appraising each other, and only after both parties are satisfied with what they see do they decide to form a partnership. I suppose I could have tried to capture this courtship, but it hardly seems right to intrude on such an intimate scene; besides, I prefer to see them ducking and diving, which is what they do best, but having done so perhaps the next best thing (especially when rises are few) is to try and guess where they will next appear.

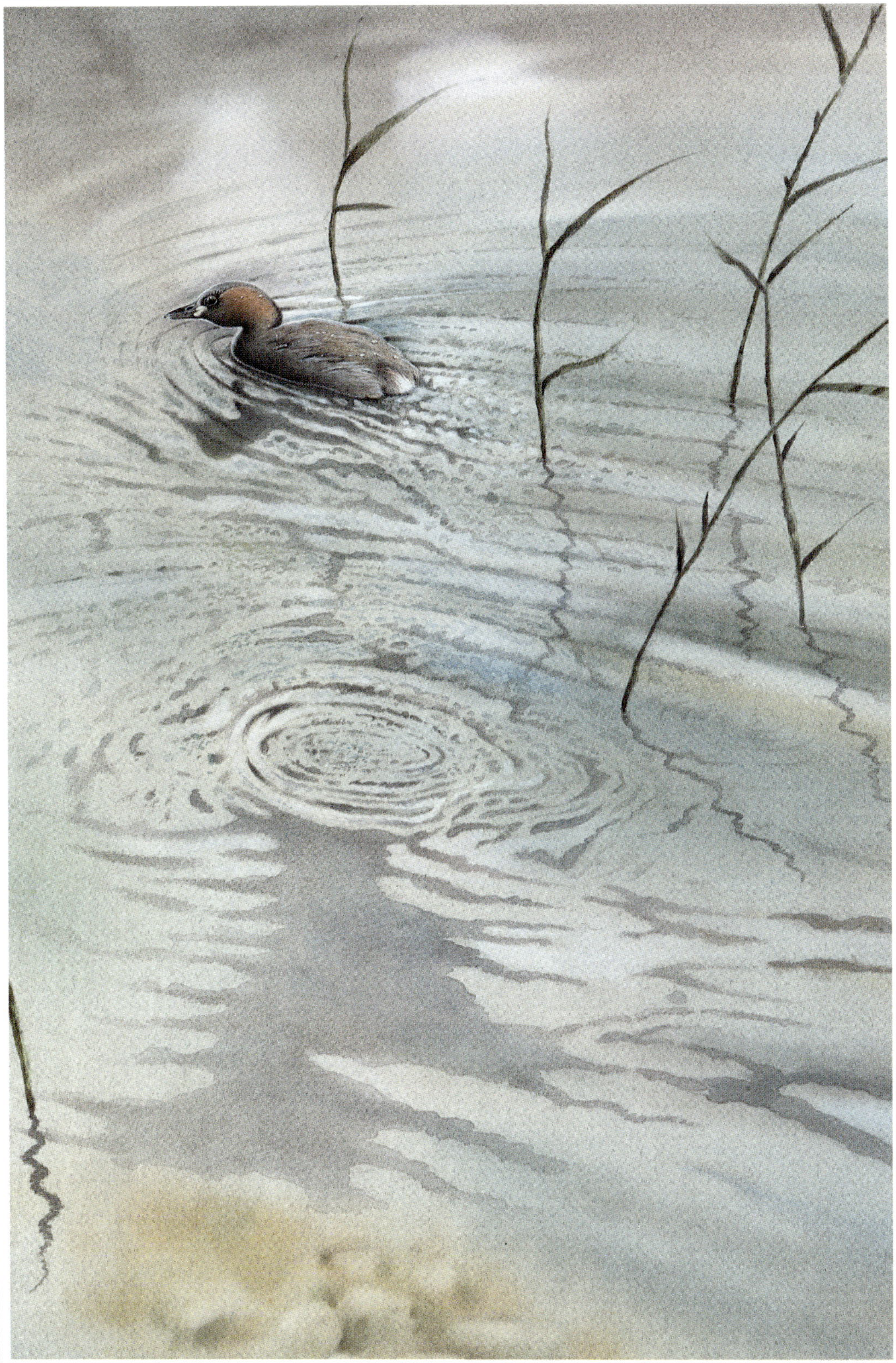

Upavon

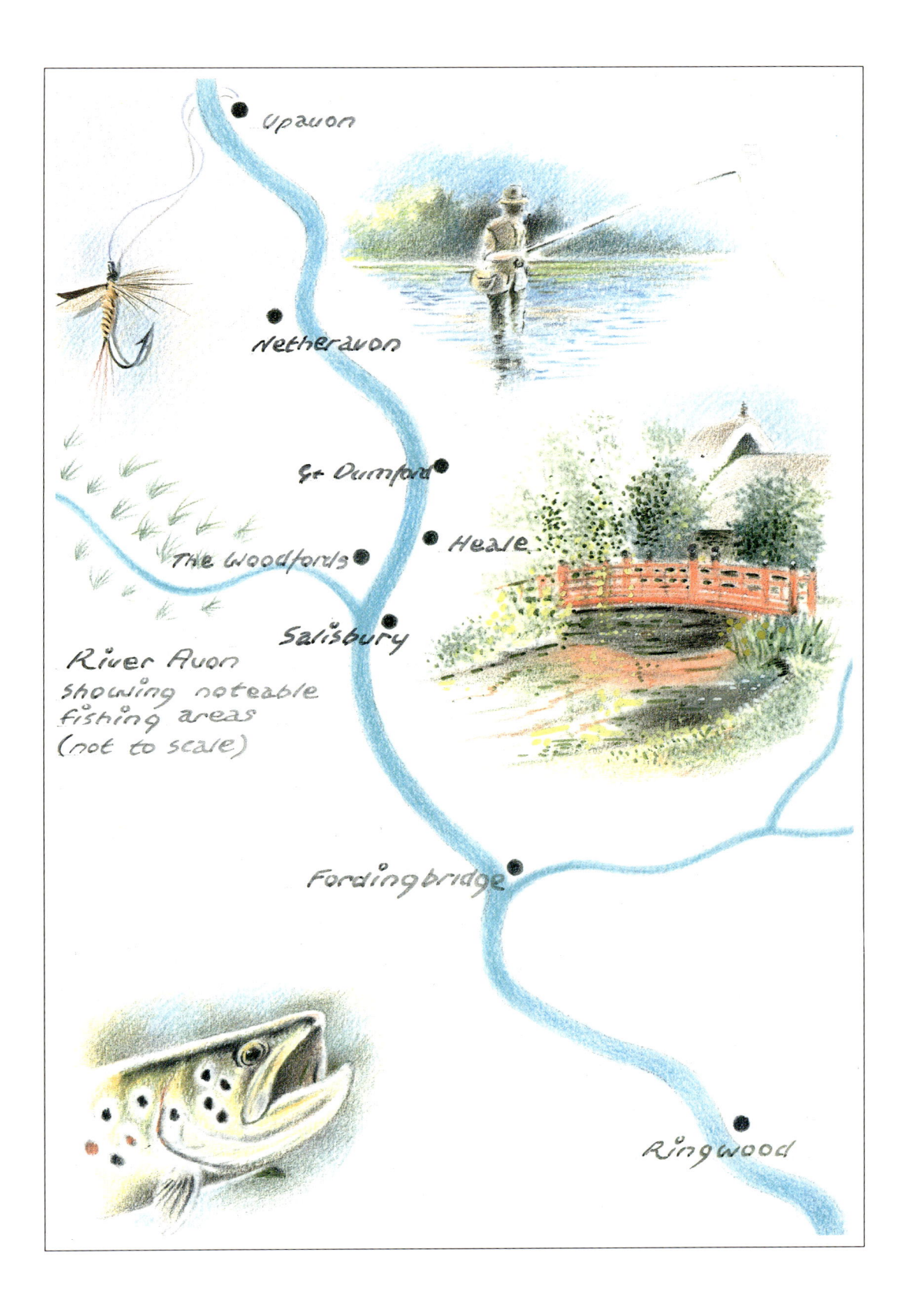

Netheravon

Gt Durnford

The Woodfords

Heale

Salisbury

River Avon
showing noteable
fishing areas
(not to scale)

Fordingbridge

Ringwood

We begin our day by fishing for grayling under a footbridge but are hampered by a muscovy duck, adamantly unmoving. I lose a brown trout which takes me behind some weed beds, then luckily, at the importuning of the producer (who thinks I need only place my line over the water to succeed in catching something), I manage to take a 1½-pounder by side-casting under a tree. Dermot releases it for me, carefully bringing the fish to hand and taking the fly by the shank to unhook it. This way, by not touching the fish, you increase its chances of survival tenfold.

At lunch we meet Simon Caine, a young craftsman who makes beautiful customised split-cane rods from £300 upwards for a 6½-foot wand, and subsidises his passion by making and repairing less magnificent pieces. We admire his genius and dedication to producing the ultimate 'state of the art' rod, then move on to an old but charming hut belonging to the Piscatorial Society – the Rod Room, full of photographs of distinguished members past and present, of fly life and of record fish. When I come into a place like this I like to muse on the continuity of fishing down the years, and to imagine what conditions were like for my fellow sportsmen of an earlier age. Were they plagued by nagging doubts about the ecological future, I wonder, or did they believe, like most Edwardians, that nothing could ever possibly change for the worse?

Tom Mottram, the keeper whom we meet next, certainly does not believe that. Several years ago he helped to monitor the effects of the first slurry pollution of the Avon, and the experience clearly bit deep. Since then he has found little to make him optimistic about the river's future. The water, he says, has unquestionably deteriorated over the past ten years: the present sea-trout runs, which he oversaw when he worked further downstream, are far less abundant than they ever used to be. Despite his Jorrocks-like appearance and his natural good humour, he cannot disguise his deep concern at the way in which the river is failing to maintain its condition throughout the season.

I would like to pursue this, but the time is not right. We leave Tom to his cutting of the bank-side weed and are about to move on when we see a fish moving just below him. It is a pike, about 1½ lb, avidly feeding on the trout fly. 'What will you do with that?' I ask Tom. 'You'll see,' he says. 'Just wait a bit.' And he goes back into his cottage, emerging with a small fibreglass rod. Digging about in an old compost heap until he finds two juicy brandling worms, he baits them on to a number 14 hook. That done to his satisfaction, he bids me stay quiet while he creeps along the bank, surprisingly smoothly and silently for such a heavy man, until he is able to dandle his tempting morsels just above the pike's nose. He lies motionless for about two minutes. The pike, too, stays seemingly inert. Suddenly, it makes a grab for the bait. Tom makes no effort to strike, but simply lets the fish swallow the worms and hook and then lifts his rod, worms, hook, fish and all on to the bank. It is a neat and economical way to master the enemy of every trout keeper.

I am amazed that the pike failed to see him. But he makes light of his skills. He often catches them like that, he says, though sometimes he snares them. Provided they are not spooked, pike will often lie motionless in a stream long enough for an experienced hand to guide the noose at the end of a long pole over the pike's head. When you have it centrally round the body, you lift it up in one easy movement and success is yours. It all seems very simple, but I somehow doubt whether a novice would manage the trick so easily. I think I would rather take my chance with the worms.

We move on, with Dermot fascinated by the riverine life as we go down to the turbines – nothing more than a big hatchery with a series of gates, overlooked by a charming old fishing hut. From there we see a fish gingerly sipping in flies from underneath the bank. 'That,' says Dermot 'is a big fish.' I trust his experience. 'Now let me see you take it.'

I will prove myself, I think. Taking a small Pheasant Tail dry-fly, I oil it well, dry it and cast carefully but unsuccessfully. I can't get the fly where I want it, and I'm worried lest I have disturbed my quarry and lost him. 'Cast across that bramble,' advises Dermot. 'Drop your fly very gently on to the leaves, then tickle it a bit and it will have to drop somewhere close. Since that particular fish is already feeding off things dropping from the overhanging vegetation, there's a good chance it will accept your little offering.' Sure enough, it does, coming up to take it very slowly and in leisurely manner from the surface of the water. As Dermot has predicted, it's a big fish, a nice firm three-pounder which, unseen by the keeper who may have objected to my action, I safely return to the water.

I had learnt a new trick and caught my fish. But I didn't want to keep it; not because I am excessively humane and sentimental, but simply because I have become increasingly anxious to preserve fly fishing, my sport and my passion, for future generations. I still do take some fish, but not many. More often, I fish with a barbless hook and return whatever I catch. I suspect that unless a few others of my 5 million or so fellow sportsmen start doing the same, there soon may not be much left to catch unless you include tame rainbows and the commercially stocked fish. If 'catch and release' can ensure that a hundred years from now our better rivers will still contain some original brownies, then I shall continue to promote it as vigorously as I can. And if the Americans, with considerably more empty acres and wild streams than we have, can nowadays take 'catch and release' for granted and practise it extensively, then we too would be wise to take it seriously.

But of that, more later. Sufficient for now to suggest that we should never fish without one eye on the future of fishing; otherwise, in the not too distant years ahead, we might well see every southern English stream denuded of its last remaining natural trout.

Overleaf: *Rainbow and Black Gnat*

Robin Armstrong

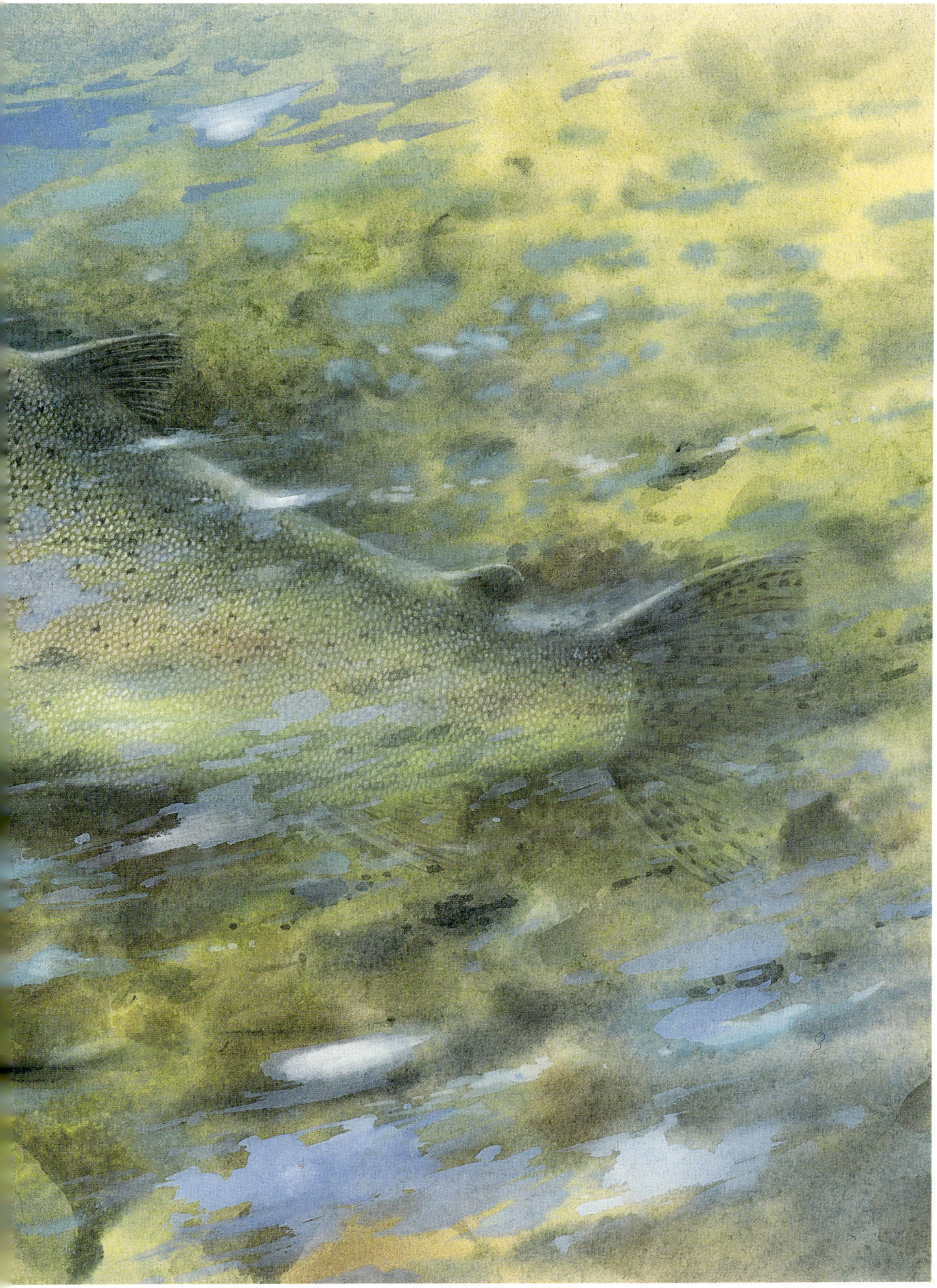

CHAPTER 8

· *Matching the Hatch* ·

YESTERDAY the Avon; before that the Test; and today the Kennet, an old hunting ground which I have fished, by courtesy of my friend David Channing-Williams, every year for several years. Normally I arrive for a few days in the mayfly season; this year, because of the early hot weather, I am too late. The heavy clouds of insect life are almost gone, and the fish are beginning to reconcile themselves to normal feeding conditions. The glut is over and the living is less easy; the fish are no longer jumping, and the angler must work rather harder than he did last week, when (I am told) trout presented themselves like mackerel from a Cornish shoal.

We are on a beat on the Craven Estate, where David has had a rod for some time. He knows the water well. It is much deeper and more gouging than the Test, and in places it floods quite fast. Fish here have a close-range chance to examine what you are offering them, so the wise man is careful about his choice of fly. Simply to bung something on the end of your line without thought about what the fish are already eating will lead to nought. You must watch what the fish are feeding on, think what you have in your fly-box which will best imitate what they are taking naturally, and then present it in such a way as to deceive your fish. Then, *perhaps*, you will succeed.

The reach I am working is long and slow, without any streaming runs or broken water. The trout are comfortable and choosy. They have ample chance to swim up and carefully examine what is on offer and reject anything strange or exotic (much as customers do at a fishmonger's).

The weather is again perfect and the water is richly stocked with rainbows which tend to feed more avidly by day than brown trout. Although not many of them are moving, the few that are in feeding mode should be easy to catch. Here, for example, is a rainbow lying at the junction of the main stream with a carrier, turning in the stream every time it takes a fly. A brown trout wouldn't do that but would stay on station, hanging on jealously to his position and using the minimum of energy to take in his food. This fish is more mobile. He is also large, and may be less easy to take than I initially thought.

Watching the fly coming off the water, there seem to be more sedges than anything else, and this is what he is probably feeding from. But rather than risk losing him by casting various flies over his nose, I shall sit quietly and watch whether he moves regularly to a given type of fly, which I can hope to imitate from my fly-box. The sedges are coming off thick and fast now, probably representing as important a source of food as the mayfly, providing nourishment throughout the season. This fish certainly relishes them, and I think I can probably make a passable imitation from a Lee Wulff pattern, tied with various hairs to imitate large insects. I prefer the one with deer hair, thick and buoyant, which I can float for a long period with a minimum of treatment.

Despite the fact that the surface film is in a poor state these days, the sedges still manage to tickle about on the water for long periods before they actually take wing. My fish is now very active. I cast upstream, over him, taking care because the stream is wide and I have only an 8-foot rod. It's covered; it's taken it, and after a battle, when it saw me early on and sped across the water on its tail, I've landed it, all 4 lb or so of hard, thick-set flesh and short tail. I tried not to let it rush about too much, for when fish are forced to fight too hard and too long they build up lactic acid in their blood system and become paralysed. So whenever I am fishing 'catch and release' I try to shorten their misery by defeating them as quickly as I can rather than letting them drive up and down until they are tired out. I release this one, as always, by holding it by the shank of the fly, with the stream gently running over its gills so that the lactic acid can slowly dissipate, allowing it to swim away happily to boast of its lucky escape.

The river further down is slow and languid. I see a heron, a protected species which Tony the keeper can no longer kill, as once he might have done. Sex, never far away in an English summer, now intrudes in the shape of mating damselflies, a more delicate sight than most of the couplings so intimately photographed by David Attenborough. I also see another fish, this time under a big tree, hard to spot and difficult to cast to. Here again, my close-focus binoculars come in useful. By watching it carefully I can find out what it is feeding on, and then, if I have the right flies with me, I can attempt to 'match the hatch'. This, I suppose, is meant to be the essence of dry-fly fishing, the skilful and artistic side of the great game, where observation, manual dexterity in shaping the fly and artistic instincts all come into careful play.

Many would deny the need for all this. It is enough, they claim, to get the rough shape of the fly the fish are feeding on; there is no need to match everything exactly. But I disagree. And not because of any theory, although a body of such theory does, I believe, exist. My belief springs from practical experience. Many times in the past I have tried flies of roughly similar size and shape to the feed but different in colour, and I have had no success. Yet when I have matched it exactly, I have won the day.

This fish is still feeding but not, as far as I can tell through my binoculars, on sedges. I study it from behind the bank, careful not to let it see me. What it seems to be taking are not black gnats but look remarkably like them. To copy them I shall take a hawthorn fly, cut off the two black legs and cast above it. Up it comes to nose about suspiciously, and then, disdainfully, turn away. Or is it taking? I

· *Kingfisher perched near the Test* ·

This painting was done at Leckford. Although I must have painted kingfishers in a hundred other places throughout the south and west of England, I only recently learned (from Charles Bingham's *The River Test* published by H.F. & G. Witherby Ltd, 1990) that Leckford is perhaps the most appropriate Hampshire place for an Armstrong to be. For Armstrongs are undoubtedly of Northumbrian origin, and the Leckford Club, according to Charles Bingham (quoting an earlier book written almost a hundred years ago by the Marquess of Granby), was founded in the eighteenth century by men travelling down from Northumberland for the mayfly season.

I am not sure why people with access to the splendid Tweed would have wanted to travel so far south for trout fishing, since even the lesser Northumbrian rivers such as the Aln, the Coquet, the Wansbeck and the coaly Tyne itself must have offered very fine sport. Perhaps they merely wished to escape their north-eastern wives, or the weather, or the dismal results of their local football team. Whatever the reason (perhaps it was simply the eternal lure of the chalk stream), it must have been a compelling one to drive them so far in such uncomfortable conditions.

One thing is certain: they did not come to see kingfishers, since although these birds may be very rare in Scotland, they can still be found by assiduous bird-watchers on most rivers on the borders. I say 'assiduous' because you need to be very tenacious to spot one, even in the warm south, because a kingfisher is somewhat smaller in real life (no more than about 7–8 inches in length) than most people imagine. Nor is it easy to paint. Unlike, say, a robin, it is distinctly uncomfortable in the presence of humans and streaks away like a bullet when disturbed, looking sometimes blue or green, sometimes red, depending on the prevailing light.

Anglers will mostly see a kingfisher perched on a tree branch or some similar vantage point above a stream or lake, waiting to dive into the water for minnows and other small fish. If they are lucky (or unlucky) they may occasionally see it, belying its beauty and behaving like a beast, cruelly beating its catch against a branch before swallowing it head first (so as to avoid entanglement with the fish scales). The kingfisher is the most brilliantly coloured of British birds and a delight to the eye of those lucky enough to spot one. But its beauty is only skin deep: beneath the technicolour its foul-tasting flesh ensures that it is not often bothered by predators.

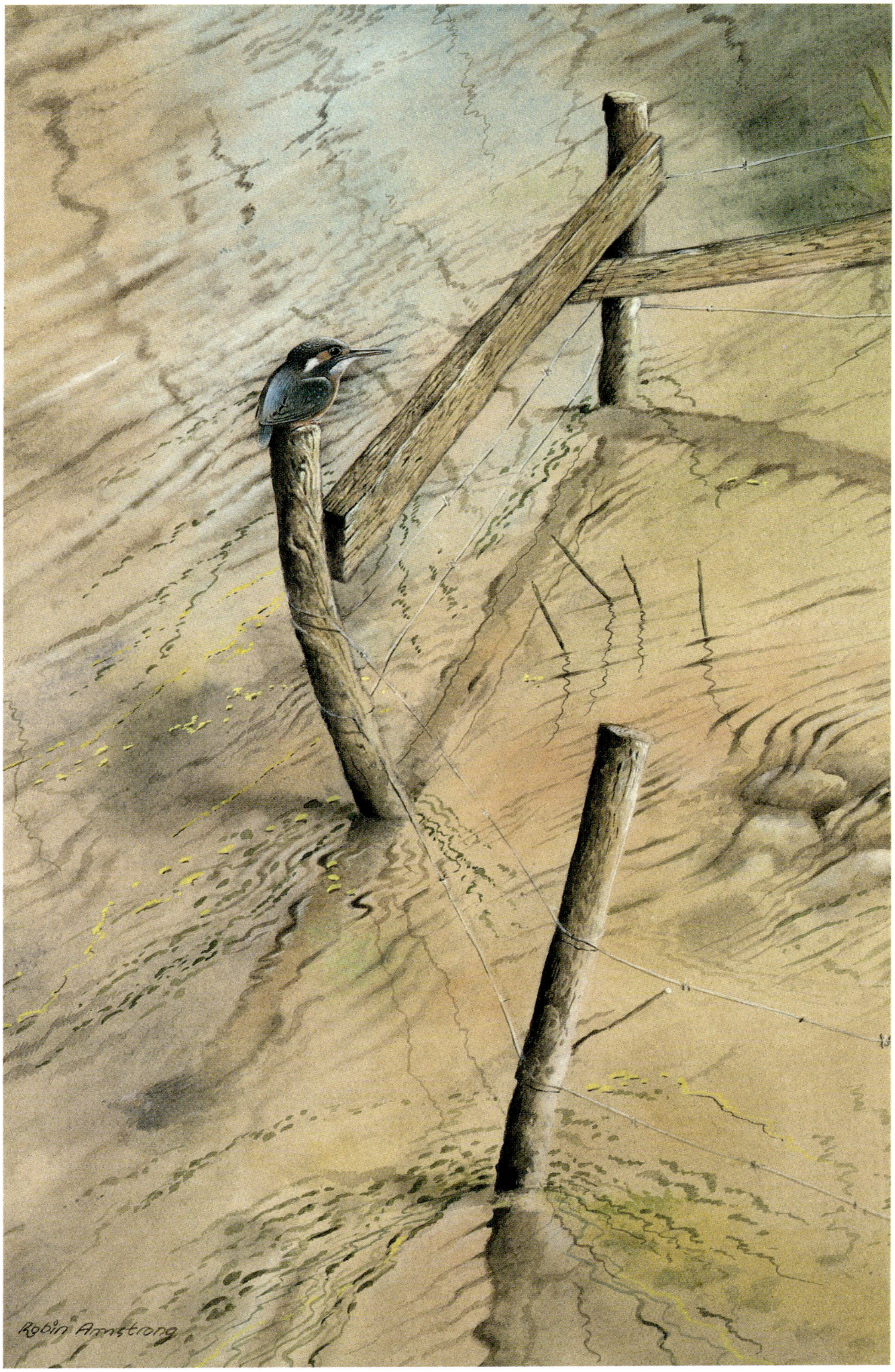
Robin Armstrong

think I pricked it, but I didn't get it. It's almost certainly a big brownie, since (characteristically) it has not moved far from its feeding station all the time I have watched it. Now, I guess, I have lost all hope of taking it for another hour or so. And that, I think ruefully, is a pity, for I'm pretty sure it is a big fish.

But where there is one, there may be others. Too impatient to wait, I move further down where sluice-gates guard a big pool, alive with a back eddy which allows you to fish upstream from a downstream cast. Here at the gate the water runs very fast along some boards where, among the plenitude of weed, some twenty or so roach, a little late for spring's mating season perhaps, are actually spawning. The sight is so rare and beautiful that it brings me up sharply with delight. I forget my fishing in the sheer wonder of it. The roach, very active and heedless of my presence although they must have seen me, present a sight to charm any painter: a kaleidoscope of translucent green and yellow bodies and red fins in the brightly whirling water.

I watch the roach for some thirty minutes, fascinated by this adventitious and rare sight. It is still hot, almost too hot to fish. Again my binoculars come in handy to watch the swarming natural life going on around me, including two big perch majestically swimming round the spawning roach, looking dangerous but not actually interfering with the latter's sport. I can also spot a trout in the eddy, moving to some smaller sorts of sedge. I try going for it with a Pheasant Tail similar to that which I used, with success, on the Avon, but this time trimming a bit off the tail to make it less fly-shaped and smaller.

I am 'matching the hatch' – doing what fly fishermen have done, if not since time immemorial, at least from Halford's day. As I wrote above, I believe it works if one can get it right, but this time I do not. I cast right over the fish but he doesn't even look at it, perhaps because he has risen to another natural fly which distracted him first. I try again but he ignores my wooing, so this time, in accord with a trick taught to me years ago, I try something in complete contrast to what he is feeding on – a big Red Sedge.

As Dermot Wilson showed me a couple of days ago, I drop it lightly on some vegetation just above him and manoeuvre it from there to let it fall lightly into the water. Success! The trout takes it, but my pleasure hardly lasts. It turns out to be very small, something rather less than half a pound, a waif of a fish, almost anorexic and hardly worth the trouble I took with it.

But then, just as I swallow my disappointment, all is commotion. My line goes taut. I feel the pull of something big, and out of the churning water, to its surprise as much as mine, I bring forth a splendid fish: no less than a 6-lb pike, fresh, fat and newly full of a small trout. I have never done this before and I doubt if I shall ever do it again. Just as the trout took my fly, the pike, lying in wait beneath the surface, must have taken the trout, only to have the fly lodge in his maxillary bone, safely away from his sharp teeth. But however I caught it, Tony the keeper will be pleased since a pike of this size could do considerable damage to his trout stocks.

The episode has made my fishing day. I suppose I should slit open the pike, rescue my trout and, if it is still living, turn it back to grow to a ripe old age and bore its grandchildren with the tale. But too many other things compete for my attention. Just below the sluice gate is a wonderfully constructed reed warbler's nest, all fine strands of reed and grass so woven as to be supported by three or four reed stems, well above the flood level. Prince Charles would approve: local materials, ecologically sound, architectured to fit in with the surrounding landscape, and user-friendly. The four or five young in it are clearly quite satisfied with the abode provided for them, and I move off quickly before mother, supporting herself on the reed stems and fussing at my intrusion, despairs of saving them.

There are more reeds further down, with another nest. But this time the occupant is a baby cuckoo, bigger and uglier than the offspring of a warbler, and signs outside the nest indicate that the warbler's eggs have been rudely ejected to make way for the parasite. Not content with taking a place, the cuckoo must always deprive others of theirs.

This is a good day for wildlife. After the warblers I see several baby moorhens, some coots' nests, built to float like rafts among the reeds, and that rare bird the hobby, not normally seen away from open downs and heaths. I watch it take a swift in mid-flight, swooping down from nowhere at high speed and making off with its prey into the westering sun. This would make a Hollywood ending to my glorious rural day if I did not have a score to settle with the trout I left earlier, pricked but undefeated under the big tree. My angler's pride is wounded; I cannot leave him victorious. After two or three hours' rest, the time has come to try him again.

This time I use a Last Chance, or the Angler's Curse, a fly which is meant to imitate the little flies that come on in the evening in these parts. Happily my fish is still there, feeding regularly and quickly off the small flies presenting themselves in the still air. I try once more to cover it, as accurately as I can, and up it comes, gently sipping in my fly. Now it's rolling over and I've caught it, perhaps teaching it to be more careful in future. I let it go, about 3½ lb of gleaming brown trout, fighting fit and firm of flesh, ready for another day. Who knows – I reflect as I pack up for the journey home – we may well meet again. The nice thing about 'catch and release' is that one can always renew acquaintance with one's old opponents.

CHAPTER 9

· *Autumn Glory* ·

A LITTLE over two and a half miles north by east from the centre of Winchester lies Abbots Worthy, little brother to the village of King's Worthy (which merits an apostrophe) and place of much delight. Here, with traffic roaring along the M3 only a quarter of a mile away, and evidence of new development all about, trout still swim in a clear, chalk-bottomed reach of the Itchen much as they must always have done: warily, but not without confidence in their ability to survive. On this particular autumn morning, with a blue sky and patchy cloud and a warm south-easterly breeze gently ruffling the surface of the water, I saw several of them: 1–1½ lb fish mainly, lazily drifting about in the shallows of the far bank, seemingly unconcerned at our inquisitive presence.

Perhaps they sensed that I had no rod with me. Perhaps they felt secure enough to defeat me even if I had been so equipped. Or perhaps they were simply getting

---

· *Stale salmon, after spawning* ·

THIS picture of a salmon exhausted after spawning was painted on the lower Test. The body of an exhausted fish like this is flabbier and less attractive than that of a salmon in peak condition, and its colour, very hard to capture in paint, is quite different from that of a fish newly returned from the sea.

No game fisherman needs a lecture on the life-cycle of the salmon or the mysteries of its peregrinations up and down its home river and distant deeps. Some day, no doubt, a marine biologist will provide answers to the questions about those travels which have intrigued salmon fishermen for generations. Meanwhile, however, lack of definitive knowledge about such large questions does not mean that we cannot solve the small ones. We do know quite a lot about how salmon feed and spawn and reproduce. We do know that salmon eat hardly at all in fresh water (although happily, they are always open to snacking at a random fly) and digest virtually nothing. Thus, it is not surprising that those which arrive early at the spawning grounds will be in poorer condition by autumn than those arriving later. Once they enter the fresh water of their home river they live off their tissue, so that the longer they have to do this the weaker they become (and the less palatable their flesh). By the time the female has scooped out a redd and laid her eggs, and the male has fertilised them, they are exhausted. Some fish will reach the sea and return again, but most cocks and many hens will die before they get to the river's mouth.

"A summer survivor, not marked
and starting to stale, waiting
for October rain"
Robin Armstrong '87

careless, with the end of the season only a few days away and the weather lovely enough to make even a trout reflect on things other than mere survival.

Years ago, some gnarled Hampshire hand must have deliberately planted chestnuts near Abbots Worthy. Judging by their siting, I doubt if the trees could simply have sprouted naturally from the shiny brown conkers small boys must have carried about with them, then as now. But whomsoever or whatsoever was responsible for them has left us a rich legacy. In the autumn sun the turning leaves were full of glorious colour – yellows, golds and browns contrasting in sumptuous profusion with the green leaves on other trees which had yet to acknowledge the time of year. I was glad to be in England and on the river, even if I wasn't fishing.

I am not familiar with the Itchen. I know it, but not well. I have fished it and had good catches from it, but I could not claim to be intimate with its special traits and idiosyncrasies. This particular morning in mid-October I had merely come with a friend to remind myself of what it looked like, and to recharge some batteries exhausted by personal problems still unsolved. I had chosen a good day. It was warm but fresh and almost spring-like; if the year was about to die, it would do so only with a struggle. Even the vegetation on the bank-side showed few signs of weariness. The reeds and grasses still seemed charged with energy, and the garden of the big house over the way looked set for summer, not for a drawing down of blinds and a lighting of winter fires.

Conditions for fishing were ideal, and I wished I had brought a rod and sought early permission to work the beat. As it was, the two of us gazing intently over the water and taking photographs of the old footbridges (for later paintings) must have looked somewhat suspicious. It was not surprising that we were accosted by Bill Loder, the ghilly, who clearly thought we were loitering with no good intent.

Things had recently been stolen from his fishing hut and he was not unnaturally leery of strangers. Who were we, he asked at once polite and wary.

We allayed his doubts in talk of common acquaintances and rivers, and listened with interest when he said he had been fishing this stretch of the Itchen for forty years. He very obviously knew it well. 'No grayling here,' he said, when I told him I thought I had seen one. 'Upstream beyond the bridge, and again further down, but never here,' he confirmed. This stretch was for trout, even if, on this particular morning, he was not having any success in catching them.

I asked him what flies he mostly used. 'Black Gnats,' he said, 'together with Black Ants enhanced with a little tail-bob.' These apparently served him well throughout the season, and he saw little reason to vary them very much. And indeed, if they produced results, why should he? There are too many fancy anglers who chop and change purely to justify the contents of their extensive (and expensive) fly-boxes. I believe that if you find something that works you should stick to it. Better to spend your time fishing than rooting about in your tackle for new temptations. On Dartmoor I find two or three old standbys quite enough to cover most conditions, and even when I'm tempted to change it's not long before I revert to tried and trusted favourites.

Bill Loder was clearly a fisherman's fisherman. He looked like one and talked like one, missing nothing in the river as we chatted on the bank-side. In the unseasonal warmth we watched fish rising to the occasional sedge, a grey wagtail dipping and diving in the carrier, and water flowing clear and strong over the chalk-stream bed. There is an elemental fascination in rivers, and it was good to know that this part of the Itchen, at least, was still moving as it always had done. But the motorway was close and vandals had already broached Bill's hut. How long before mindless oafs wrecked the footbridges and tore down the trees?

We went back to the car and drove on, to the waters of the Test's Leckford Estate, past green meadows and woodlands ablaze in a thousand autumn tints, and old cottages made bright by money from outside the area. Tomorrow's ghillies may not be able to afford to live near the beats they are meant to conserve; tomorrow's countrymen may be mere weekenders, two-day rustics who cannot tell a Rabbit's Foot from a Gold Ribbed Hare's Ear. But for now, the rivers, meadows and trees still look to be in good heart, and village life seems to go on much as it ever did.

We were bound for luncheon at a well-known pub, the Mayfly, close by the river at Testcombe not far from Stockbridge. The food turned out to be plain but good, and the beer was well kept. It was almost warm enough to have sat outside and watched the dimpling trout rejoice in the end-of-season sunshine. I began to think, traitorously, of moving from my moorland streams to Hampshire, where nature is softer than in west Devon and the fish are plumper and more accessible. In this Test Valley one is never far from alluring stretches of river and stream,

· *Brown trout in green water* ·

SOMETIMES even the Test is discoloured (though not necessarily polluted) with run-off. I painted this trout as much for the water as for the fish, being attracted by the depth of rich green in a river which is usually clear. As experienced anglers might guess, having watched and weighed colours for years, getting the water right can often be the most difficult part of fish painting. The whole authenticity of a fish picture is lost if the feel of the water is not properly reproduced. However demanding it is to capture the complex colouring of a leaping salmon or the right line of a standing heron, satisfactory pools and ripples and depths of tone in painting water present an even greater challenge.

and splendid prospects of rich meadows and trees. Bird life, too, is more variegated and profuse, pubs and houses have a warmer look and the land is less stark.

Each habitat offers its own charms, I suppose, and I can relish both, but when I'm in chalk-stream country I probably do find more subjects to paint and more sociability in the fishing. Dartmoor offers far fewer sudden little vistas; its countryside is less domestic and on a larger scale, and man-made architectural delights are rare. To anyone with imagination, hut-circles dating from Neolithic times have a bleak fascination, but one lot is much like another, and so, except to those familiar with them, are most tors.

I am therefore charmed that every time I revisit the country around Stockbridge I always find a myriad of surprises: tantalising glimpses of river through the foliage of a drooping willow; attractive houses mellowed by time; wooden footbridges, somehow very appropriate to their purpose; unkempt meadows, and old mills telling plainly of a comfortable rural English past. Perhaps I am growing tired of Dartmoor's harshness. Perhaps (for although I spent most of my childhood in London, I was born in Hampshire) I am simply being drawn once again to my subconscious roots. Whatever it is, a thousand subjects in this lush county tempt me to try painting them.

It is time to move. We turn from walking the riverbanks and make our way back to Devon. It is too late, this year, to fish the Itchen but I shall, God willing, be back next season to sample the delights of a river which I have so far known only in part, and then briefly. Most of my chalk-stream experience up to now has been with the Test; after our wanderings today I think I need to widen my vision. I suspect that every yard of these Hampshire rivers is worth exploring, and wherever I can explore them I shall. I may not, like Bill Loder, achieve a full forty years, but it is something to be aimed at; it seems to me that a man could do much worse with his spare time than to use it strolling these gentle paths in pursuit of chalk-stream trout. Test or Avon, Kennet, Itchen or a dozen other of the meandering streams which Walton may have walked (and over which, I like to think, his spirit still presides) – all provide not only excellent sport but welcome relief from the cares of this unquiet age.

CHAPTER 10

· *Chalk Stream and Cherrybrook* ·

Long before I set eyes on Avon or Kennet, Test or Itchen, countless numbers of fishermen must have explored every inch of them; countless more have devoted hundreds of hours to their management and conservation, and countless others have fished them more successfully than I have. What, then, are my qualifications for attempting this didactic comparison of chalk-stream and other trout rivers?

The answer, I fear, is 'fewer than I would wish'. I can only plead that if no one did anything until he was perfectly qualified, nothing would ever get written and no debate would ever begin. Let me simply say, therefore, that if I am relatively immature on chalk streams, I can lay claim to a little knowledge, acquired over more than fifteen years as a river warden, of the streams of upper Dartmoor. And perhaps my experiences as an average fisherman on these streams, striving to improve his performance, may be closer than those of a cup-winning guru to the sympathies of other average fishermen.

But enough of modesty. If I lack brilliance, I have at least rubbed shoulders with the very best of Dartmoor's fishermen and watched them at their skilful work. And I have walked the banks of every mile of Dartmoor's many boulder-filled streams and even tried, at times, to count some of the fish in them. I have known mornings, evenings and afternoons when the West Country skies have thunder-clapped open for rain to soak me to my freezing marrow, and I have fished among stark tors on days when Hampshire men would hardly dare venture out of doors. I have experienced the full range of disparate moods the wide and beautiful moor can offer, and explored each of its streams and leats from source to sea.

Fishing here is very different from fishing on a chalk stream. Our waters are often dark and swirling, full of eddies where they break against the many rocks, and mysterious brown pools under peaty banks that the flow has bypassed. After a sudden storm the water runs straight off the hills, transforming a quiet river into a torrent and a gentle stream into a dangerous obstacle. Even when the sun shines and the air is still, the brooks of the upper moor never reflect the calm of their surroundings. They are always full of motion, chuckling and burbling downwards to the coastal valleys, protecting their hardy denizens by the speed of their flow. Trout here are rarely fat and never lazy. They move fast, travel light and wait upon no man. Life at this level is pretty elemental. Food is scarce and has to be worked for – great, easily picked feasts of hatching mayfly are rarely seen. The full and fat tables of the chalk streams are unknown in these parts, and nature's handouts, such as the rich bonuses of Hampshire nymph, arrive but rarely. This is the part of the world where trout need to get on their bikes if they are to survive; any fish hoping to find a well-stocked personal suite in which to live out his languid days must think again.

Our trout, in short, are active and wiry. They have to be to survive. They are rarely very big since they feed only frugally and exercise more than most, having to move about to find places in which to play when the water is low (many trout streams are tinier than outsiders ever imagine) and new refuges from the fast-rushing floods when the water is high. But for all their relative lack of water space, they're not always easy to see; only experience teaches one where to look for them, and how best they may be tackled.

Moorland streams, of course, eventually merge into rivers. And the rivers become more civilised and domesticated the nearer they are to the estuary. Fishing for trout towards the mouths of the Tavy and the Dart, for example, even if it involves techniques other than those commonly used on the Test, is an equally well-mannered discipline. But fishing for hill trout near the source of those rivers is a very different matter. The fishing about which I write here is fishing on the moor, where the weather is inconstant and subject to sudden changes; where the streams are fringed by boulder and bog; where human habitation is markedly rare, and the ambience is elemental and sometimes harsh. This is the very opposite of fishing on the chalk streams.

In theory, perhaps, it should be harder to take a trout from a stream like the Cherrybrook, north of the Tavistock to Ashburton Road (the B3357, for anyone looking for it), than from a rich branch of the Test. And so, for anyone not used to such a stream, it might be. For a start, the newcomer might have difficulty adjusting to the terrain. Anyone used to a manicured bank or a well-kept path would find the Dartmoor going tough. He might find it hard to juggle his rod as he sought a handhold to stop himself slipping. He might find it difficult not to snag his line among rocks, or avoid stepping on to a bright green knoll which turns out to be composed of pure mud beneath the moss. But if he copes with this, will he know where to look for fish?

If he is wise, he will spend his first visit with a friend who knows the stream. No amount of reading up beforehand will help so much as this, since there are few landmarks and knowledge of the ground can properly be gained not from a map, but only by walking it. And even when he comes to a possible lie, finding fish in these small brooks is not easy for anyone but those who are practised in reading the water. Assuming, however, that all has been overcome and that the newcomer is ready to make his first cast, how will he then fare? The answer lies in his fundamental fishing skills and instincts, as it always does. He who fishes

Overleaf: *Fresh salmon*

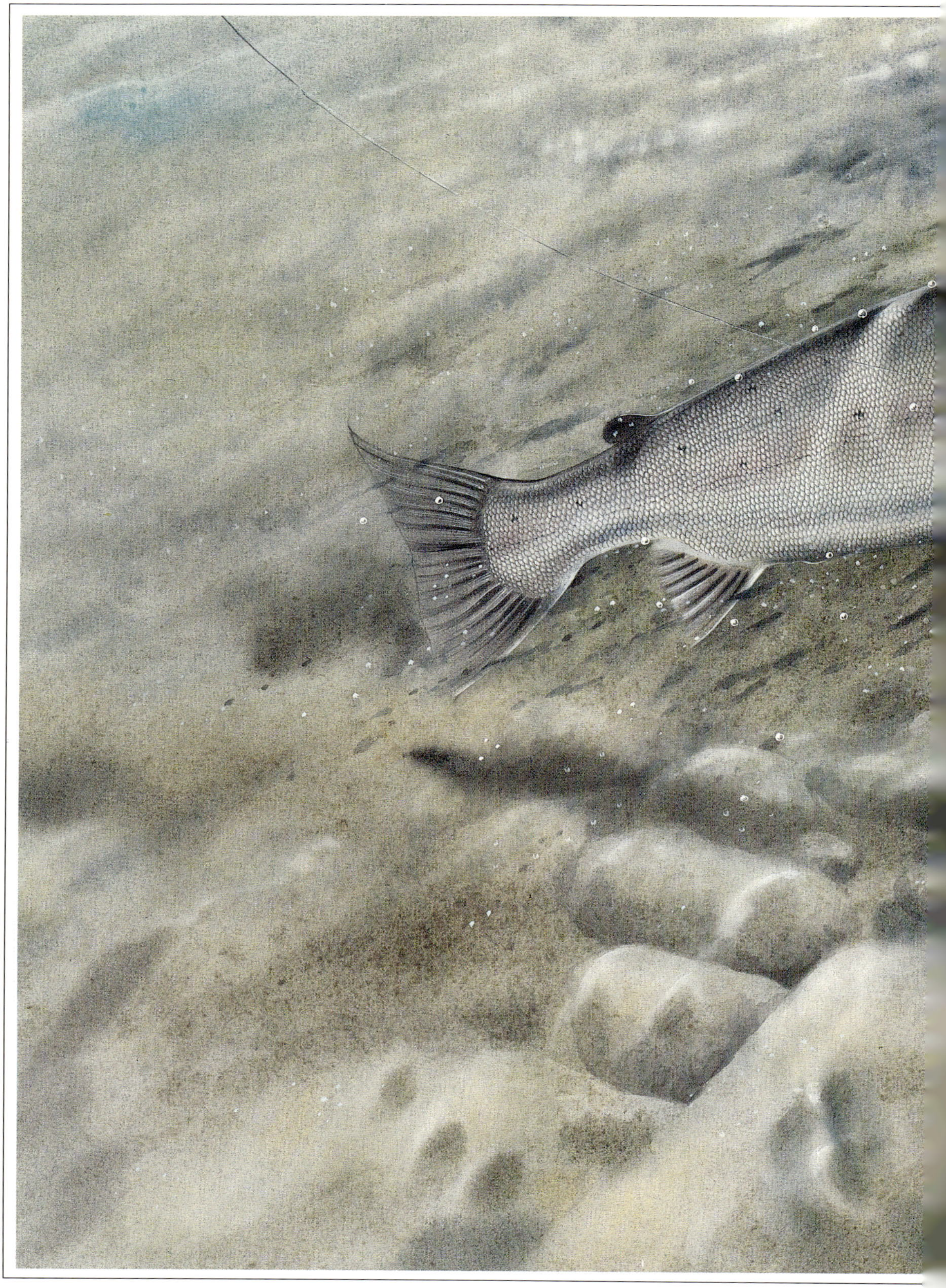

Taking up the slack — don't strike yet!
Robin Armstrong '87

well in one river can always learn, provided he is not too impatient or too proud to take local advice, to do well in another.

Dartmoor trout may seem hard to take because they are hard to find in any great number. And having less insect life settling on their waters' surface, they are less likely to be seen feasting themselves from surface duns. But because they have less on which to feed, they cannot afford to pass by on the other side when something is offered to them. Provided you can present your fly attractively and put it down with a modicum of dexterity, your quarry may well attempt to take it. What fish can afford to ignore a possible snack when the next offering may be long in coming? It is the poor who snatch their food and the rich who exercise restraint. A chalk-stream trout, gorged with all the wealth of insects with which it is often surrounded, will pick and choose what it eats since it can afford to be cautious. Amid plenty, it has no need to gobble up the first thing it sees.

As a general rule, a properly baited hook dropped from a handline into a barrel of live mackerel will catch you a fish. The catching of a trout, however, takes a little more effort. Over the centuries, a lot of thought has gone into the question of how best, with rod and line, it can be persuaded to swop the security of its watery home for the dubious charms of a creel. By and large, and subject to many exceptions, the outcome of that thought is agreement that the dry-fly is more successful than the wet-fly on gin-clear streams, and that the wet-fly is the more successful on the darker, less placid waters of the moors. That, at least, is the rule as taught to me, and having stated it baldly in black and white, I shall no doubt never sleep again for people ringing me up to say I talk nonsense.

At one time, of course, all fly fishing was wet-fly fishing, and the dry-fly really took over on chalk streams only when Halford and his disciples found that they could catch more fish by this method. Later still, when dry-fly men began to assume the mantle of the fishing world's heaven-born, they began to propagate the perverse notion that because the dry-fly method required more skill to make it effective, it was therefore a more sporting and gentlemanly method than the wet-fly. In other words, some fishermen claimed to use it not because it worked but because it made catching fish more difficult. They were thinking, I suppose, along lines similar to those which decree that sitting birds should not be shot.

I can understand the analogy, but I cannot accept it. The finer points of which method is more sporting than the other escape me. I use the dry-fly on chalk streams because it works, because I can see my fish taking my fly and I don't have any problems in hooking it. Having picked the fly appropriate to the hatch, I make a brilliant cast and drop it, delicately and skilfully, with all the confidence of the true artist, about a foot upstream of my chosen fish, letting it drift gently down until my quarry takes it (or so I dream; in reality the delicacy, the skill, the confidence and the artistry escape me far too often, and I have to start all over again, by which time the fish have retired, I am very hungry and the pubs have closed).

The vision is a nice one. There is no doubt that dry-fly fishing is an elegant vocation, but the fact remains that the wet-fly method demands just as much skill and usually makes more sense. Since trout spend most of their time feeding underwater rather than from the surface, it would be logical to think that wet-fly fishing ought more often to produce results. And on most streams, most of the time, it does, whether one is fishing upstream with flies or nymphs or downstream with lures.

For the vast majority of anglers, chalk-stream fishing is going to remain an out-of-reach pipe dream, for reasons of either distance or expense. But it can be obtained if one puts aside a few days and a few twenty-pound notes to secure it. If you have friends whose beats you can share, you are fortunate indeed; if you have not, you need to take more trouble. But your trouble will be more than recompensed by the unique experience. To stand on the Test or the Itchen on a summer evening, the air scented by freshly mown grass, the quiet river ruffled by nothing more than the ripples caused by a rising trout, is as close to paradise as most of us will ever know. As the 'broad sun sinks down in its tranquillity', you can almost touch the stillness. Here, surely, is the very soul of this sceptred isle.

Whatever their methodological predilections, all trout men should try one of the chalk streams at least once, preferably with a split-cane rod and an old reel, just to feel at one with the nineteenth-century pioneers of modern dry-fly methods, and to understand the high side of trout fishing. Like the Ritz Hotel the Test is open to all, at a price, and the price is worth paying. It will certainly buy you a fishing memory you are unlikely to forget.

CHAPTER 11

· Riverside Diversions ·

Only the single-minded angler succeeds, say the experts, and he who wastes his bank-side time watching the antics of a dipper or the comings and goings of a common shrew is unlikely to go home bowed under with the weight of his catch. The complete angler needs to address his mind solely to the matter of fishing; let his thoughts wander to other things and he is lost. Stalking and casting,

---

· Sea-trout leaping at night ·

Even when there is no harvest moon to illumine the river, as there was when I painted this picture, you can still tell the presence of a leaping sea-trout from the sound it makes when it plops back into the water. I became familiar with this sound when I was a water-bailiff in Devon, lying in night-time wait on the riverbank for reported poachers, straining to distinguish the creaks and snuffles of animal life from those of human intruders.

This picture is the product of a warm August midnight, star-filled and almost as bright as day. The graceful arching of the fish is characteristic and a wonderful sight, never to be forgotten. Sea-trout are now becoming relatively rare on the upper reaches of the chalk streams, and I promised not to reveal where I drew this one. I am told that there are still places where they run well, although 'running well' is a comparative term since numbers are said to be only about one-twentieth of what they once were, at least on the Test. On the Itchen, sea-trout varying in size between some 3½ and 11 lb come in early and go out early, moving very fast. They are shy fish and hard to catch in the day-time; I was advised by one expert to fish for them at night with a Great Bucktail.

Sea-trout have been badly affected by inshore trawlers, some of which relentlessly scrape up everything in their search for greater profits. They have also been adversely affected by increasing water abstraction and pollution and by lack of supervision of unlicensed fishing. One theory suggests that sea-trout come in cycles of ten years and that we are soon due for a new surge. I shall believe this only when more detailed research, backed up by my own or my friends' experiences, confirms it.

Sea-trout make fine eating, and so will always command a premium price. Because of that, so long as human nature remains unchanged, they will always present an irresistible temptation to poachers. If only genetic engineering could bring grayling to adapt, like trout, to salt water, then our estuaries might fill again with enough worthwhile fish to satisfy everyone.

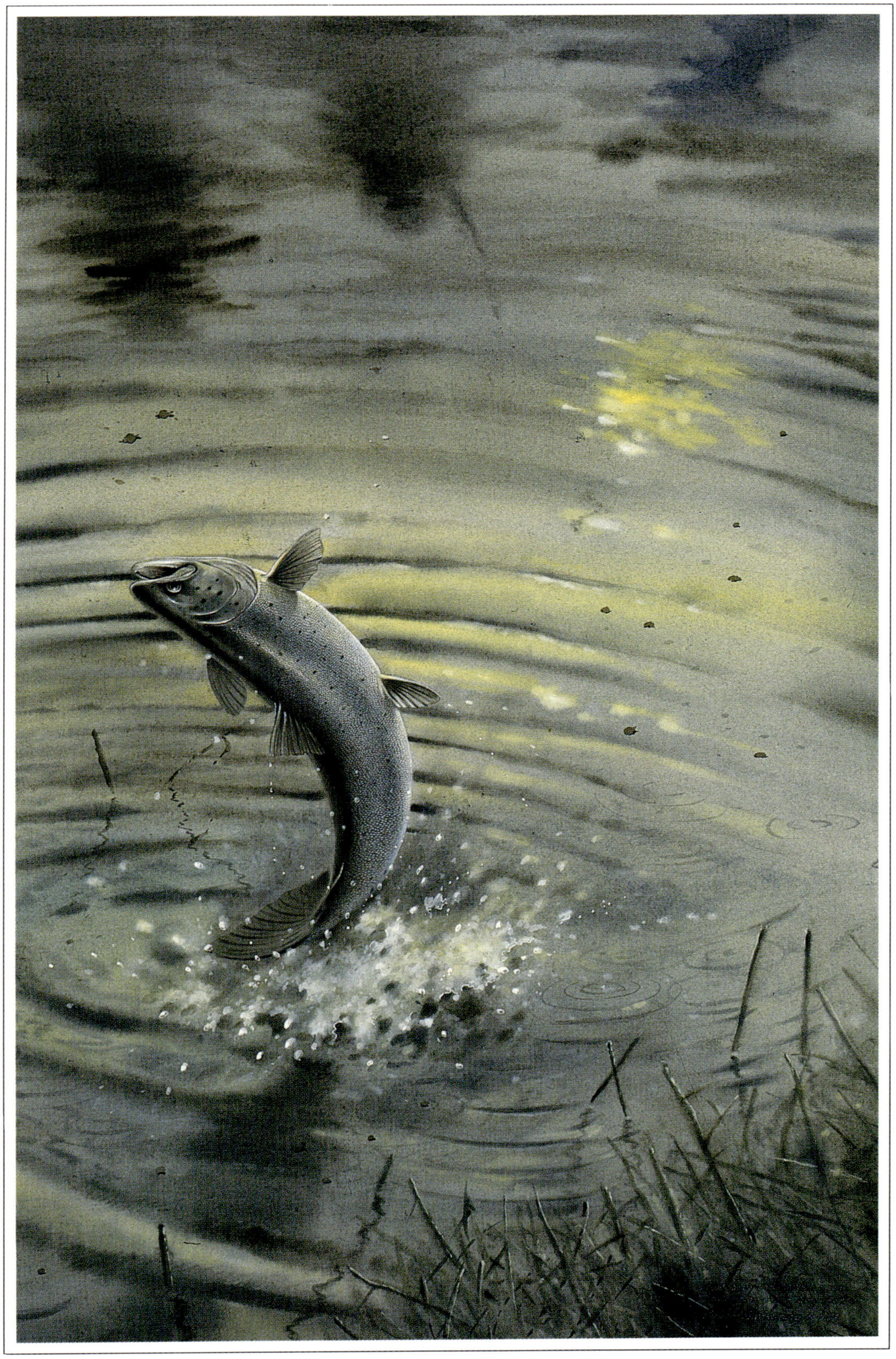

choosing flies and baits, studying weather and water and the vagaries of insect life are subjects that merit all one's concentrated attention, otherwise the fish that matters will get away and the day will be lost. Anyone lucky enough to be invited to fish for trout on a richly stocked chalk stream should have no thought for anything other than the task in hand. All else is an irrelevance, and the sighting of a rare bird, far from its normal habitat, should distract him not one whit from his solemn objective.

But I am not sure if fishing alone can ever secure every last whit of my attention, except perhaps when I actually have a catch to bring home. There is so much other natural life going on around a river that I cannot help but be intrigued and diverted by it. Fish are just one aspect of river life; the insects, the butterflies, the bank-side voles all have walk-on parts in a rounded production in which all share the credits. Thus birds, which are never far away from an angler's beat, are for me one of the greatest of fishing's many delights. I can name most of the common ones (and many of the uncommon). For many years I have enjoyed studying them, sketching them and reading about them, so that when nothing much is happening in the water and trout are proving hard to find, I'm happy to take a break from fishing and simply bird-watch. There are few parts of Britain where, if you're observant enough, you cannot see some form of interesting avian behaviour.

I confess that not all birds lighten the spirits all of the time. On a lowering day, with the sky steel-grey and a mass of heavy dark cloud threatening rain, some of them can repel and send shivers through the least imaginative mind. On such a day (and they are common on my Dartmoor home ground), when I'm fishing the upper Tavy and the tors, wreathed in mist, loom larger than they really are, I have often chilled at the sight of ravens picking the bones of a dead sheep and looking aggressive enough to attack me for my live flesh.

These birds, big, black and sinister, are hardly even kissing cousins to a cheerful robin or an ever-busy dipper, and they have nothing in common, except their airworthiness, with the bright wagtails and kingfishers which grace Hampshire's domesticated streams. Nowadays at least, ravens are mostly birds of the wild moor – large and somewhat unfriendly, harsh-voiced and ugly – and are quite out of place near the gentle ambience of a chalk stream. On the Test and Itchen I expect to see prettier and more amiable forms of bird-life, although anyone who has ever watched a kingfisher beating its catch against an overhanging branch must wonder if anything in nature could be more red in tooth and cruel in claw. It seems a universal rule that most birds, however beautiful, are more than happy to tear apart whatever will feed them and their offspring.

And this, I suppose, applies also to one of my favourite birds, the heron. I have seen more of them on the lower reaches of Dartmoor's rivers than I have on the chalk streams of Hampshire, but wherever I come across them they delight me.

Simply to catch a glimpse of one standing in the shallows, unmoving and infinitely patient, is a wonderful sight. Only the most crabbed of anglers could resent the small threat that herons represent to the average fisherman's day. What they take in fish, they more than give back in sheer beauty. I, at least, am not so much of a hunter that I can put my own desire for a heavy catch above their survival. I believe that nature's inherent tendency is towards a balance of conflicting interests; if nobody shot herons and nobody fished for trout, both species would manage to survive. I'm glad that the law now protects them and that keepers can no longer kill them with impunity, since I am sure there is more than enough room, even on today's overcrowded streams, for both them and us.

One old belief, recorded in at least one reputable bird book, which held that fish are attracted to the oils in a heron's feet, prompted some older anglers to grease their lines with the bird's fat. I suspect they would be as well off using low-cholesterol margarine, and that rather than killing a heron in order to employ the dubious allure of its body fat, the fisherman might gain more from watching it work. Herons are successful because, in exceptionally large measure, they have the attributes of all successful anglers: a good eye for the right water, an instinct for when to strike, and infinite patience.

Patience and a good eye are also the qualities one needs to spot birds. When I first began to take an interest in wildlife other than fish, I often heard (but failed to see) the birds that surrounded me. Indeed, I learned only later that the more tuneful the bird-song, the less likely I was to see the bird, since melody often goes hand in hand with drab, hard-to-distinguish plumage. But I persevered and learned my birds by watching, photographing and sketching them, checking my observations from museum specimens rather than books, and I have never regretted the time spent doing this. Many a fruitless angling day has been enriched by seeing a rare bird, and simply being able to identify the common or garden varieties which proliferate in southern England brings me great pleasure. In those parts of Europe where everything feathered that flies is shot, the absence of friendly bird-life is very noticeable.

Painting birds can be harder than painting fish; both are elusive and frequently fast-moving. Swifts have been timed (I'm not quite sure how) at over 50 miles an hour, and peregrine falcons are listed, in the *Guinness Book of Answers*, as reaching over 80, which is a good deal faster than a fast-moving salmon at a mere 23. But even if both bird and fish are seen only fleetingly, at least you have more chance to check on all the details of a fish because it will often be one you subsequently catch and photograph.

With birds I also use photographs to supplement my memory of a particular cameo – the antics of a daring robin perhaps, flaunting himself with no thought of potential danger; or a wagtail, busily searching the banks for insect life with which to feed its bawling young. For me, such sights are as much a part of fishing as catching fish; he who can resolutely ignore them must indeed be dull of soul and deficient in imagination. While I would agree that anybody who has paid to occupy the bank of a chalk stream would be a fool not to put fishing first, he would also be foolish to ignore the other delights chalk streams can offer. With most as rich in birds and wildlife as they are in good trout, the wise man will take in everything.

But if I can enjoy the benign presence of wagtail and bunting, reed warbler and even the common sparrow at my fishing feasts, what of ducks? Many anglers, I know, regard them with a prejudiced eye, sharing none of the love for them evinced by small children and those happy adults who were brought up on Beatrix Potter. But I don't object to them. 'From troubles of this world,' said the poet, 'I turn to ducks.' The prescription is a good one. Few sights are more soothing than a female mallard followed in stately procession by her brood; few induce greater peace, or calm city nerves so well. If ducks do ruin fisheries or spoil the angler's sport, I have little evidence of it. In my view we can live with them, provided we don't look for too many fish in too small a stretch, nor greedily measure out our angling lives by the sole criterion of large catches. As with herons, I think that ducks immeasurably enhance any riverscape, giving far more to fishermen than they ever take away.

But perhaps I am prejudiced. I like natural fishing on natural streams, surrounded by wildlife of every sort. Even when I know that civilisation is just around the corner, I prefer tricky rivers and their attendant carriers to over-stocked ponds where the main draw is a guarantee of good catches. If I shot, I would prefer rough shooting for the pot to the formal shooting of driven birds in organised parties. Since my own feelings on these things are inchoate and felt rather than the outcome of rational thought, I find them hard to explain. But what they amount to, I suppose, is that I believe in going along with nature rather than trying to fight it – or, in this specific case, in trying to live with herons and ducks without slaughtering them for a temporary gain in fish numbers. I believe that most natural creatures have a purpose, and that if we over-react when they occasionally inconvenience us we do so at our long-term peril. I like birds of all kinds, even the predators, and I get enormous joy from watching them, noting their idiosyncrasies, observing their family lives and simply seeing them at work collecting food, and at what sometimes looks like pure play.

Do birds ever play without any purpose other than sheer enjoyment? I like to believe they do, no matter what the experts may say. But whatever the reasons for their various wheelings and hoppings and plungings and divings, they contribute greatly to my pleasure during a day on the river, calming the unquiet mind almost as effectively as a Chopin étude or a glass of good wine. So if you don't take much notice of bird-life, I recommend that you start doing so. At the very least, the practice may compensate for those hours when nothing takes, or for those long days when your only memory is of the one that got away.

CHAPTER 12

Victoriana and the Cult of the 'Dray-Flay'

Though new discoveries are the common order of every present day, and the scientific possibilities for man's achievement seem boundless, I doubt if we have ever been more obsessed by nostalgia. Edwardian diaries, Victorian designs and age-worn artefacts have suddenly become very fashionable. People who spend their working lives at the leading edge of high technology are among the first to restore old houses to their original state and to fill them with antiques; the craftsmen forgers and distressers have never been so busy.

Fishermen are not immune to this manic but understandable desire to laud the past. Otherwise sensible and successful men will scorn the latest in carbon-fibre technology to drool over old cane rods and engraved reels. Large sums will change hands for nineteenth-century fly-boxes which will never be used. A time-embalmed trout, lovingly caught by some long-dead sporting parson and boldly mounted into a mahogany display case, might fetch several hundred pounds in today's inflated markets, and an old creel even more. Even a small gadget like the Hardy's 'Curate', with tweezers, oil-bottle and gut cutter, produced by the thousand, might now cost some four hundred times more than the 30 pence at which it was sold in the early years of this century. I doubt if there has ever been a time when fishermen have shown greater interest in the origins and development of angling, nor paid more to collect examples of the tackle used by earlier practitioners of their sport.

I can understand this, since I collect and sometimes deal in such stuff myself. There is a special and compelling fascination in handling old tackle – marvelling at the inventiveness and craftsmanship which went into the making of, say, a nineteenth-century reel, and imagining who used it and on which rivers. I have no special feeling for old things merely because they are old, since rubbish is rubbish however long it survives. But old angling artefacts are different; so many of them were truly well made and properly balanced, nicely meeting the demands of both aesthetics and function. Possessing such examples of good workmanship is a delight in itself, but there is an additional pleasure, for anglers, in dreaming about the days when a particular item was first introduced. Nostalgia is not a profitable emotion, but it's an enjoyable one in which to indulge occasionally. Old rods, fly-boxes and the rest always make me, at least, dream of days when life was slower and hay was stacked in the fields rather than packed into huge rolls, and rivers flowed without fear of death by poisoning.

I suppose that, given my interest in angling's bygones, I ought to study the history of tackle. But it is less detailed history than a general feel for well-crafted fishing impedimenta and the people who commissioned it that seizes me. As a painter I am always interested in shapes and colours, and intrigued by the look of things. And I'm particularly drawn to the stuff produced in the latter half of the last century, when fly fishing in its modern form really began and fishermen's needs were served by small family manufacturers, often with their own retail shops. Bits of tackle from this age bring to life those early sepia photographs of knickerbockered fishermen working the same chalk streams as we do, and help to reinforce my fancy of being at one with a very old mystery. However sophisticated fishing becomes, however many fishing journals and books attempt to unravel its secrets, however inventive the advances in rods and reels, the essence remains what it has always been – a human in one element pitting his skills against a tiny creature in another. And this simple contest, undertaken with different equipment and in thousands of different circumstances on rivers all over the world, has formed the basis of a consuming passion for millions of people throughout civilised time. Collecting old tackle makes me feel part of this long and happy tradition.

In the confident 'then' of eighty or a hundred years ago, as much as in the more unsettled 'now' of today, intense argument about the relative merits of different tackle no doubt took up much of the fishing season's evenings in Hampshire inns. Then, as now, everyone nurtured his own harmless prejudices about which particular brands of rods and lines and flies and hooks would lead to success. But the Victorians themselves, I suspect, harboured rather less reverence towards old things than we do. They were keen to buy the very latest equipment; they welcomed innovation; they applauded, and bought, all the new fishing accessories which Hardy Brothers, in their London and North British Works at Alnwick, were turning out almost every month. From the 'Patent "Perfect" Fly Reel' (modestly billed in their catalogue as 'Without doubt the lightest and most perfect Fly Reel the world has ever seen') through Pocket Line Greasers to Patent Lockfast Rod Joints, this firm, and its competitors, were producing a wealth of innovative tackle and fishing accessories for which the market, clearly, was extremely buoyant, even if some of the items now seem somewhat esoteric.

There are many more anglers today than there were then, when fly fishing at least was a sport more or less confined to the middling rich, and much more tackle is now produced than ever before. Arguably, too, today's tackle is more reliable, better designed and probably cheaper, in relative terms, than it has ever been. But the urge to amass bits of fishing impedimenta from the past, and to hang on to discarded rods and reels, remains. I have already explained my own obsessions, but why so many others share my fascination I am not sure – I guess for the same reason that many of us prefer the look of steam trains to diesels, or old Bentleys to their modern counterparts. The newer models of almost everything may be more efficient, but they are rarely so lovingly crafted or so often successful in combining good looks with utility. Cane, silk, brass and silver are somehow more in keeping with fly fishing, particularly chalk-stream fly fishing, than plastic and different sorts of fibre, and anything hand-made seems to strike a chord in many anglers' hearts. Fishing, after all, is one of the most elemental of pastimes, with deeper roots than most; it is hardly surprising if many anglers, however innovative they may be in their business lives, are traditionalists in their moments off duty.

Americans are not proof against this same nostalgia about fishing times past. Indeed, some of the prices they are prepared to pay for the products of an earlier age are higher than those we in Britain would contemplate. The turn of the century saw an equal boom in the supply of fishing exotica in the United States as in this country. Things on offer ranged from Izaak Walton Fishing Suits, through Lathes for Amateur Rod Makers to lists of flies as long as telephone directories. And the makers were as proud of their products as ours were. Mr Thomas H. Chubb, for example, who set up shop with a model factory on the banks of the improbably named Ompompanoosuc River in Vermont, devoted a good deal of his catalogue not just to his extensive product list but to showing the details of his factory's operations. Like many manufacturers of the time, his business clearly meant more to him than a source of income: it was something that produced goods of which he could be very proud, and which latter-day American collectors are equally proud to own.

Until the late 1950s, when fibreglass rods first began to come on to the market in any number, split-cane (or more properly split-bamboo) had been the favourite rod of most fly fishers, being light and flexible without losing much in the way of strength. With one of these a skilful angler could cover almost as much water, with considerably less effort, as if he had been using a longer, stiff two-hander. And with the rod (at least for anyone rich enough) would have been any one of a number of posh reels from among the latest offerings of the Hardy Brothers, or Charles Farlow of 191 The Strand, London, or any one of several other firms offering a wealth of tackle choice and a high degree of personal service. On both sides of the Atlantic fishing was becoming a very popular middle-class sport, subject (particularly in Britain) to all the proper conventions and unwritten rules by which Victorian society liked to govern itself.

It was also beginning to adopt, on lines which ran parallel to those of other aspects of late Victorian and early Edwardian social life, its own little snobberies. And one of them was the cult of the dry-fly. It was much later that the delightfully erudite Richard Walker put a wickedly satirical vowel into those words, and the

Hooked rainbow

Chalk-stream brown trout

new spelling has remained with me ever since. 'Dray-flay' was not perhaps the pronunciation used by the Edwardians, but it was probably they who began to promote the notion that dry-fly fishing was in some sense more sporting and socially acceptable than other kinds.

I'm sorry they did, since there are some foolish people who have continued to propagate this pernicious gospel. It is one thing to use the dry-fly because you genuinely enjoy the challenge of landing your fly in the right place, but to pretend that this is in some way a superior art to that of wet-fly fishing is just silly.

I have met several 'dray-flay' people who try to give their particular predilection some special status, and, like Walker, I have little time for them. Walker was a mild and tolerant man, patient with duffers and kind to learners, but he disliked the pretentious; like the great Walton, he saw angling as bringing men together, not dividing them. Any attempt to rank one technique above another, and, even worse, to imbue it with social significance, would have met with his contemptuous disapproval. Halford would have felt the same.

No one who has tried to take any sort of trout from any sort of stream with any sort of rod and line would ever pretend that it is an easy task. But neither would he pretend that the skills needed to undertake it successfully can be acquired by only a privileged few, after a lifetime of study. The truth is that anyone prepared to read, and to supplement his reading with plenty of practical work, can quickly become a perfectly competent angler.

Assuming that the newcomer has been properly advised as to the right gear, and that he is prepared to listen and learn, his path to greatness is not as stony as some self-appointed guardians of the craft would have him believe. For the chalk streams he follows the advice of Izaak Walton and learns to 'study to be quiet' at all times. He then practises casting, and learns to read his chosen water. On flies he takes local advice, and if he is wise decides to carry with him only the half-dozen patterns that will have been recommended to him. More than this, despite the allure of a hundred other varieties, he will politely eschew.

The objective of the fisherman is to catch fish, and provided he stops short of explosives, or poisons, or illegal netting, he is entitled to use whatever enticement he likes (within the limits laid down for the stretch of river on which he is working) in order to attain his sporting end. I once met someone who claimed he could hypnotise fish by lying, with a snorkel, face down in the river and out-staring them (which I suppose a Houghton man might shy away from). But this and my given exceptions apart, I take the view that most methods are equally acceptable so long as they involve a rod and a line and a licensed eccentric at one end of it.

Most Victorian gurus of the dry-fly method certainly thought so. Halford and his contemporaries used dry-flies rather than wet because they found them more efficient. But when conditions demanded the use of the wet-fly, they used that, and without compunction. It was only their class-conscious grandchildren who began to associate the dry with the high, and to look down somewhat on the rest of angling mankind. But, as Walker pointed out, various forms of fly fishing had been going on for over two thousand years, with preceding generations simply adopting whatever method was best for the prevailing circumstances. The only real explanation (although it fell far short of a justification) for equating the dry-fly method with the upper crust of fishing's followers was that it suited pellucid chalk streams. And fishing on such streams, as most of us are painfully aware, is somewhat more expensive than fishing elsewhere.

Every sport develops. The governing bodies become more institutionalised and the rules governing it become more complex. People spend more money on equipment and the right clothes. The facilities become more expensive, and the oldest and most exclusive venues become almost inaccessible to all but holders of ancient rights and the new extremely rich. Even trout fishing, a pursuit once confined to quiet countrymen or the knowledgeable among their town cousins, has now become a subject for 'corporate entertainment' and 'management incentive packages'. Buses, I am told, ferry important clients to the delights of a lake where even the newest of tyros can be guaranteed a catch, and the most important clients can sample the gourmet food and plenteous drink in a lakeside restaurant.

It all seems very distant from the days when Halford and his cronies were developing chalk-stream fishing and perfecting techniques which are now commonplace. But I wonder, sometimes, if it really is. As people grow richer they not unnaturally want to sample the pleasures which were once out of their reach. Fishing of every sort now commands a very large following, and what most of us regard as the best of fishing – namely that with various forms of fly – will naturally attract the more socially ambitious. Victorian businessmen were just as much Johnny Come Latelies to the chalk streams as some of their counterparts are today, and their ambitions – to be accepted as equals by squire and laird and to follow the same country pursuits – were similar. Perhaps we shall never rid mankind of a disposition to rank things in a social pecking order, so let us welcome the pretentious along with everyone else. Sooner or later they will settle down into liking the sport for its own sake. Meanwhile, we may also have to accept that dry-fly fishing on chalk streams, if not elsewhere, may indeed soon become the exclusive preserve of the rich, and that the rest of us can expect to enjoy it only rarely.

CHAPTER 13

· Future Conditional ·

In summer, when laden motor cars pour along Hampshire's main trunk roads in unbroken lines, and the approaches to every town reveal yet more office blocks and shopping centres, I'm sometimes haunted by the prospect of what southern England might so easily become: one vast extended suburb, with avenues of tidy houses and identical trees all pollarded and trimmed, and the old rivers tamed and penned by concrete banks. Here in this new Utopia, plastic herons will stand guard over municipal goldfish pools; butterflies will fly only in designated air space, marshalled by uniformed fauna wardens; and somewhere in the background will be the sound of amplified musak, emanating from a leisure lake made from old gravel pits.

Happily, my pessimism rarely lasts. The sun comes out; my painting begins to go well, and I'm invited to try a new stretch of river; my brisker self reappears and tells me that my forebodings are simply not justified. Even on the worst assumptions of population growth, there will still be plenty of genuine countryside left for our children to enjoy. Even 5 million new houses would take up little more than 2 per cent of the English land mass.

But the comforting statistics do not mean that we need not be concerned. Potentially harmful demands of many sorts are being pressed on the environment every new day, threatening plant and animal life of every sort. If trout fishing, among a host of other country pursuits, is to thrive in anything like today's form, some trends need to be watched with a very wary eye indeed.

Even if there will still be plenty of countryside available to the next generation, there may not be too much river space. Already, 5 million people in Britain are thought to fish, and I suspect, from my experience as a river warden, that the number within this awesome total who are dedicated to the pursuit of wild trout may be growing. And this despite the price of day-tickets on a chalk stream rising to anything between £75 and £100 a day, and the cost of fishing rights to 100 yards of the same stream reaching £100,000. It is sobering to think that there are individuals and clubs already prepared to pay so much for such limited (and presumably, by west Devon standards, crowded) beats. To an outsider, the scales of a chalk-stream trout must look more like gold plate than silver, but even the high cost does not seem to be quelling the demand from people wanting to enjoy traditional river fishing for brown trout in fashionable locations.

The sheer numbers of fishermen with increasing leisure time to devote to their hobby may place the greatest pressure on all our rivers, and particularly on chalk

· *Salmon netted at sea, near Southampton* ·

The increase in numbers of estuary poachers using micro-mono-filament nets is one of the biggest threats to the future of chalk-stream salmon as well as to sea-trout. Illegal netsmen are not concerned with the future; their aim is short-term profit with no thought of tomorrow, and the damage they do is incalculable. There is no simple way to combat them. To cover all the sea-room available to them demands a heavy and expensive presence of bailiffs in fast boats. To deter them (and this is arguable) probably requires more deterrent sentences than have been meted out in the past.

Without a greater policing effort, I doubt if netting will ever be completely controlled. As a water-bailiff I spent many frustrating nights on estuary duty in Devon, knowing that poaching was taking place but unable to catch those who were doing it. My sympathies go with those who do the same cold and often dangerous job in Hampshire.

streams. Some people's fishing aspirations may be satisfied by the opening of new lake fisheries, and the kind of up-market social facilities such fisheries have begun to offer. But many will not be satisfied with less than the real thing. Almost inevitably, the demand for stream fishing, and its cost, are likely to rise sharply. I doubt if many of our children will ever know, at least on the chalk streams, whole days on quiet reaches without a fellow angler anywhere in sight.

But in what state will the quiet reaches themselves be, twenty years from now? Will not our rivers, as in the Old Testament lines, have turned to blood, and the fish in them have died, and the rivers themselves have begun to stink? Without the recent interest we have taken in conservation, perhaps our rural streams might have gone the way of our industrial rivers. For it now seems that the huge amounts of slurry and sludge emanating from the rich dairy lands of north Cheshire play a significant part in the pollution of the Mersey. The less than perfect condition of that majestic river is no longer thought to be entirely the result of its being used as an urban and industrial sewer; innocent-seeming pastoral agriculture is also a contributor to the mess.

We are all, I think, (with some serious reservations about our willingness to fund our convictions) belated conservationists, aware of the environment in which we live and prepared to protest against ill-conceived developments. But the pollution brought on by some developments is not always obvious, nor does it necessarily harm the immediate neighbourhood. The effects of new buildings on the quality (and quantity) of water in our rivers are often appreciated only after the development has taken place. A proposal which looks innocuous enough for one area might easily turn out to have disastrous consequences for a river many miles away. We can all read and understand development plans, but few of us are competent to visualise their effects on local water resources.

In the past, this was a part of the planning process which tended, perhaps, to be neglected or treated perfunctorily. Rural planners and councillors, pressed by an influx of townsfolk to build new houses and create new jobs, only rarely gave serious thought to the effects of their decisions on local rivers. Until recently, non-fishermen took water for granted; rivers rolled down to the sea much as they had always done, perhaps getting a little dirtier and running a little lower every year but not so much that people other than anglers ever noticed. And if they did, few succeeded in securing urgent change. Even now, when many policies are green and most councillors are incorruptible, I doubt if any river's long-term well-being will ever be given priority consideration in planning discussions until local anglers themselves, preferably with access to geomorphological advice, begin to lobby more coherently for their own interests.

Meanwhile, as pressures grow on all our river systems, I suspect that chalk streams, being relatively slow-flowing and dependent on the aquifer, may prove more vulnerable than other rivers. But just as no two trout men would ever agree on the best fly for a particular stream, neither would they agree about which pressures are the most malign. I am therefore open to argument when I say that near the top of my own little list I must put water abstraction. Since neither rainfall nor the capacity of the aquifer has changed over the years, it seems self-evident that the increasing demands made by people and industry must sooner or later be reflected in a depleted reservoir and diminished rivers. How much diminished needs to be studied in detail, as do the effects of the diminution. Meanwhile, there is anecdotal evidence from anglers that abstraction accounts, at least in part, for much-reduced salmon and sea-trout runs and many fewer natural fish.

One newspaper report (in late 1990) claimed that some 84 million gallons, a quarter of the Test's daily flow, are abstracted from the river, and all but some 5 million gallons are returned to it. But to my simple mind, if the abstraction takes place upstream and the water is returned many miles downstream, the effects on the deprived section are going to be exactly as if all the water were removed permanently. If the scientists maintain that water abstraction has no harmful effects on any part of the river, clearly the onus is on them to prove their case. Anglers will find it hard to believe that demands on both surface and underground water supplies are not contributing to silting, reduced salmon-trout runs and fewer natural fish.

There are, of course, many other contributory factors to this decline, mostly well known and commonly discussed even if not yet sufficiently researched. What importance one attaches to each depends partially on one's own experience, which is why accidental and not so accidental discharge of farm slurry also rates highly in my personal catalogue of harmful pollutants. In quantity, slurry can kill off almost every living creature over a large stretch of river. In some incidents in the West Country I have seen a whole season's crop of young fish simply wiped out,

---

· *Wild brown trout on the Bourne* ·
(overleaf)

THERE are at least two Bournes (apart from the one from which no traveller returns) that I know about in connection with fishing. One, where this drawing was made, is in Wiltshire, flowing from the north-north-east to join the Avon near Salisbury, and the other is in Hampshire. The Wiltshire Bourne is truly a 'winterbourne' for a good deal of its length, drying up in summer almost everywhere north of Idmiston. Further south, it still produces good trout.

The Hampshire Bourne was made famous by Harry Plunket-Greene almost seventy years ago in his book *Where the Bright Waters Meet*, a classic fishing memoir telling of his experiences earlier in the century of a small Hampshire stream (the old Ordnance Survey called it a 'rivulet') which runs into the Test some three miles below the Basingstoke–Andover railway line. It's a wonderful book, beautifully written, which will vividly bring to all but the insensate the feeling of a gentler and less crowded rural England. I could quote extensively from Greene and be sure to delight every reader, but it would be better for you to discover the treasures of reminiscence in his book direct from its own pages.

Had I thought, when I first began to sketch and paint fish, to make a brief note of the circumstances of each and every brown trout I tried to capture with pencil and brush, I would by now have filled a large number of notebooks. But even now, that first sight of a new 'brownie' never fails to fill me with elation. I shall go on painting them until my fingers fall off.

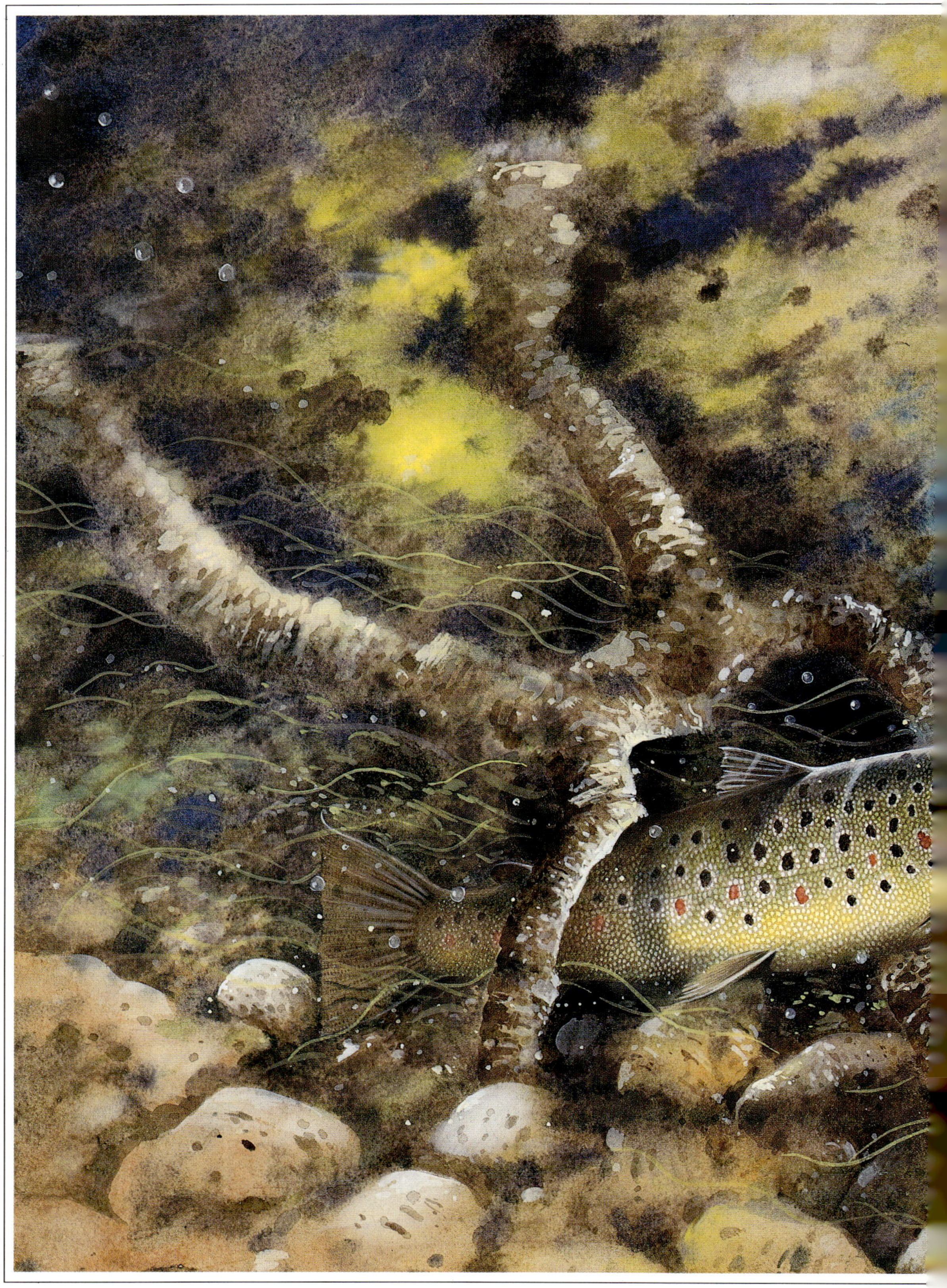

Robin Armstrong

and spawning beds ruined for years to come. Outside the obvious industrial pollutants on our main commercial rivers, 'farm waste', according to Lord Crickhowell, chairman of the National Rivers Authority, 'is the biggest cause of river pollution in many parts of the country, and nothing less than a national strategy will help overcome the problem'.

I agree with him, and so will most anglers. But I suggest we need to recognise that the problem is not merely one of deliberate law-breaking. Significantly, Lord Crickhowell also noted that of the 10,000 farm discharges given consent over an earlier year, many were 'unsatisfactory', which presumably means that even the law-abiding fail to reach the standards which ought to prevail. We have to assume that if illegal discharges were stamped out altogether we should still need answers to the question of how to deal effectively with the harmful waste products of intensive cattle and pig rearing. Perhaps even more importantly, we need to solve the long-term problems presented by nitrates and pesticides which remain in the soil and run off into our rivers years after they were first sprayed.

There are other dangers to the quality of river life that only the largest rivers, and not always those, can withstand with equanimity – oil and tar which run off from roads, for example, and accidental discharges from local sewage works. Even in such a strong river as west Devon's Tavy, fast-flowing and fish-supportive under most conditions, I have watched helplessly as dozens of dead trout and salmon rose to the surface after one relatively small outpouring of part-treated effluent into its depleted summer waters. The old Water Authority itself was responsible for this accident, which supports my point that rivers, even to those who are responsible for their upkeep, are too often seen, albeit unconsciously, as handy conduits for clearing up our inconvenient waste.

Chalk streams face their own special and further hazards, since it is on or near them that natural fish are threatened by the possible fouling of downstream water from the proliferation of trout farms; by stocked rainbows which escape and eat large quantities of fly; by the flooding of water meadows, which kills off potential insect life; by careless or neglectful weed cutting, which can ruin the fishing in the lower reaches; and, not least, by poor policing. I was told by one regular angler that it was quite common, at least until recently, for downstream netsmen and anglers not to be asked to show their licences, and for those rare ones of whom such credentials were demanded never to be requested to display what they had actually caught. One wonders how many undersized fish escaped detection because of this, and what effect their taking had on future stocks.

Trout, salmon and sea-trout share the same risks in the rivers, but the latter two fish are in even greater peril at sea. Given the reckless scraping of the sea-bottom by inshore trawlers, illegal netting by professional poachers and illicit or accidental marine oil discharges, it seems surprising that either of these species ever survives to reach their spawning grounds. Yet they do, even if runs are said to have declined dramatically from the earlier years of this century. And there are – just – some hopeful signs that the authorities (at least on the Test and the Itchen) are now intent on atoning for past ineptitudes by adopting programmes to increase salmon numbers. They are also engaging in serious research on pollution, fish numbers and much else, and I applaud their efforts. But my cheers are still limited, since the threats to the chalk streams' fishing future are many while the measures to counter them are relatively few.

Angling is a serious pastime for a vast number of people. But it is not a sport with a high public profile; its interests are not as readily promoted as those of athletics or football, and it receives very little financial support. In practice, angling clubs very largely look after themselves, and individual anglers pay their own way through buying rights or day-tickets wherever they can. Unlike the situation in America, the theoretical home of individual ownership, where fishing is very often free (although they do have catch regulations) and anyone can fish rivers provided they don't trespass in order to reach them, the riverine rights in Britain are mostly privately owned and jealously guarded. Our freedom to roam and fish is restricted; that of the 58 million or so American fishermen is wide and generous. They have national parks which alone cover almost twice the area of England and Wales, and hundreds if not thousands of rivers and streams, thirty-eight of which exceed 600 miles in length with the longest, Mississippi–Missouri, stretching for an almost unimaginable 3700 miles. Of their twenty-four lakes with an area of 150 square miles or more, one, Lake Superior (shared with Canada), covers almost 32,000 square miles, four times the size of Wales. For a nation with only four times our population, this is a lot of good, fishable water.

Compared with all this, Britain's total fishing resources are few and the length of our chalk streams infinitesimal. Space on all of them is at a premium, and of that which is encompassed by the Test a goodly part belongs to the Houghton Club, whose membership is out of reach of all but one in ten thousand trout men. Perhaps, therefore, one should ask if the upkeep of the chalk streams is important. If public money is to be spent on our rivers, should it be spent on improving a river on which the mass of anglers will never be able to afford to fish?

The question has already been answered. At the first public meeting of the National Rivers Authority, the chairman promised to maintain the Test 'as if it were a great work of art or music', giving it a status above all other rivers. It is a status well deserved. The Test is unique. It offers splendid fly fishing in some of the most beautiful of English rural surroundings and affords enormous pleasure even to those who simply walk its banks and look down into its limpid waters. It should, it must, be preserved, cherished and maintained as well as any fine country house or ancient church. But whether it can remain for ever the strict preserve of the few is another matter. My guess is that this question will not remain unasked for much longer.

· *Tailpiece* ·

SIXTY and more years ago, on the final page of his classic book *A Summer on the Test*, J.W. Hills, sometime Financial Secretary to His Majesty's Treasury and a very gentil, parfait angler, said that although fishing on the upper Test had changed for the worse, the waters of the middle stretches at Stockbridge and those lower down at Mottisfont and Kimbridge had 'on the whole improved' from what he remembered of them when he first fished them forty years earlier. 'There is,' he concluded, 'no need to fear the future.'

This was an apposite end to so joyful a book, and I wish I could close my own with such happy certainty. Sadly I cannot, because from all I have seen, heard and read I would question whether today's Test has improved on the Test of the 1950s. And unlike Hills I am less than sanguine about its future, believing that it will not be a better river than it is today unless we energetically apply the lessons learnt from past mistakes.

I am no historian and I do not pretend to know exactly, or even within fifty years, when we seriously began to despoil the heritage of our rivers. I would guess the date at somewhere near the beginning of the nineteenth century, when the Industrial Revolution was beginning to get purposefully under way and heavily polluting forges and shipyards, petrochemical plants, papermills and processing factories of every sort, all of which used and abused large volumes of water, began to grow along the banks of Tyne and Tame, Tees and Mersey. Over the years, all those rivers which supported large conurbations gradually became almost lifeless. Even the coarsest of coarse fish could barely survive in them, until by the late 1940s we almost forgot that they had once enjoyed thriving salmon runs and a lively trout population.

The traditional southern chalk streams knew little of the depredations experienced by their northern counterparts. Few industrial plants blotted the Hampshire countryside; coal mines were not dug into the Wiltshire turf, and factories, apart from one relatively small paper mill, did not spring up along the banks of the Test. Halford and his friends, and those who succeeded them, were mildly concerned at the sewage from new country houses, but their main preoccupations lay with weed cutting and stocking, not the toxins from some factory.

Trout fishing up to the time of Hills was the sport of gentlemen, or at least those rich enough to be accepted as gentlemen. Gentlemen owned the rights; gentlemen administered them; and gentlemen's servants looked after the immediate business of warning off poachers, keeping the river in good heart and seeing that sport was ever ready for their masters' pleasure. The problems facing

Sea-trout just off the tide

chalk-stream anglers were for the most part trivial, and nothing much marred the angling joys of those who could afford the rents and fees. It was a halcyon world, close knit and fairly exclusive; those within it enjoyed good fishing in wonderful surroundings with no thoughts of a polluted tomorrow.

Ironically, while our industrial rivers are getting cleaner, our rural streams are now coming under threats only slightly less menacing than those from early manufacturing industry. Some threats, indeed, may be even more pervasive. We may be able to reduce the numbers of accidental or deliberate spillages of farm slurry by tougher policing and higher penalties, but the dangers from excessive nitrates and pesticides are more difficult to control since we cannot easily trace their origins, and the evil they do lives long after them: the after-effects of a spray applied today may not become evident in a river until years ahead.

For the first time, too, the interests of landowner and fishermen are becoming markedly diverse. What the former did in the past rarely affected the rivers; what he does now, by way of draining meadows, heavy fertilising and extensive spraying, may damage fish-life to an intolerable degree. In today's world profit often rules, and short-term self-interest takes precedence over long-term principle. If some farmers are now beginning to spare the hedge and stop spoiling the meadow, there are many others who cannot afford to put ecology before economics. The establishment of Environmentally Sensitive Areas (ESAs) along parts of the Test, where farmers are paid to eschew modern and more efficient farming methods for the sake of preservation, is a small step forward, but not a giant stride. Development on their edges can have almost as ill an effect as development within the ESAs themselves.

And development, at the risk of repeating an old message, may be inescapable. So, too, may the use of fertilisers. When these result in increased yields and lower food prices, governments of every sort must be tempted to acquiesce in their use, even if the long-term result is some reduction in fish stocks and the quality of game fishing. After all, consumers outnumber fishermen, and anyway, in the long term we are all dead. Few governments think much further ahead than the next election.

The chalk streams are a national asset, but by and large they are privately owned and not too openly accessible to the masses. It would therefore be unrealistic to assume that the public would always support anglers in any campaign to keep those streams exactly as they are. And not all the 5 million or so who are said to fish would necessarily fight on behalf of the chalk-stream purists, who are often seen as privileged and exclusive. If the Test and her sisters are to be saved in their present form, then a lot more organisation and effort must go into saving them. And a lot more consideration will need to be given to opening up banks and water to a public which is presently looked upon, by many anglers, as the enemy.

TAILPIECE

Up to now, the Test and its environs have remained largely unspoilt. Where changes have taken place they have been gentle changes, hardly damaging the age-old harmonies of village and countryside nor disturbing the timeless flow of ancient streams. But things may soon alter. Basingstoke and Andover have the dubious distinctions of being among the fastest-growing towns in England. Commuters now look to live in places which would earlier have been ruled out as too distant from their workplaces. No one can doubt that their demands for housing will soon be felt in every village within twenty miles of the main urban centres; no one can doubt that hungry property men must already have their eyes on the development potential of every one of a thousand green fields on the peripheries of each small settlement.

Demand for local sources of building materials will grow, and as farming incomes are squeezed, new uses will be sought for fields which up to now have remained much the same since Norman times. But above all else will be the immediate pressures of more people who are affluent, leisured and determined to enjoy life, full of restless demands for pleasure grounds, picnic sites, places to park and lakes for noisy boats with engines fuelled by oil and petrol which will inevitably get into the river systems.

I do not pass judgement on this. Everyone has an equal right to enjoyment in his own way, provided he doesn't impinge too obviously on the rights of others. I merely record what I think might become a reality. What can be done about it, if anything can be done, I do not know. What I do know is that the demand for rural pleasures, and the expansion of the town into villages instead of (as of old) into leafy suburbs, are new phenomena which could have disastrous effects on a river and environment as delicate as the Test and the Test Valley. In this land, settlements and river system are uniquely interdependent; it would be foolish to believe that an expansion of the former would not have some effects on the latter.

The Test is unique. At least, everybody says it is unique, and people do come from all over the world to fish it. But according to Mick Lunn, quoted in the *Daily Telegraph* in November 1990, 'modern man is sucking it up and mucking it about'. One American fly fisherman, commenting in June 1989 on the colour of the Test water and the number of 'hatchery dummies' (stocked rainbow trout which are not natural to the river), was quoted by Conrad Voss Bark as saying that we 'have neglected and abused one of the most famous rivers in the world'. If his comment had held no grain of truth, I doubt if a respected angling correspondent of *The Times* would have bothered to quote him. It is more likely that the anonymous American is not alone, and that he reflects the fears about the future held by many others.

If those fears are valid, they must concern us all. There are still some other places in southern England where streams and meadows remain undefiled, where trees and hedges are still being tended and cherished, where birds still sing and fish still swim much as they always have. But few of them – perhaps none of them – have a trout river like the Test running for forty miles or so through their tranquil hearts. To preserve this river and its surrounds as close to perfection as we can must surely be important.

Anglers cannot and should not resist every proposed change in regional life. Population in this part of Hampshire will almost certainly increase and the pattern of general economic activity, as well as agriculture, will need to alter to meet changing demands. New building and road development are almost inevitable, and I would not oppose it. But if I lived in the Test Valley I should do my best to see that it was properly directed away from the most precious reaches of river and stream. And as an angler I would try to cooperate with others to anticipate how we could best reconcile our interests with those of the general public.

But first, perhaps, we need to have more than mere anecdotal evidence as to what is happening to the chalk streams. We need more solid research on water levels and water quality, on fish stocks and the effects of fish farms, on pollution and the growth of weed – on a dozen more matters of which at present we speak only in conjecture. And if we are to exercise any authority as an interest group, we need to give rather more support to the Anglers' Cooperative Association than we presently do.

Somewhere in Britain, quietly living exemplary lives, there are 5 million fishermen whose affairs and grievances still receive little more press and public attention than those of tiddleywinks players. And that, perhaps (for we are a nostalgic lot and dislike change), is exactly how some sections of the game-fishers' old guard would wish things to remain. But I very much doubt if things can so remain, at least if we are serious about maintaining and improving the standards of the best of our rivers. One day, perhaps, like the suppliers to other sports, those tackle manufacturers who gratefully relieve us of our surplus funds might be persuaded to contribute more to specific items of fishing research. If angling is to survive and thrive, such support is certainly needed. But until that frabjous day, we can only salute the owners, river wardens and clubs who still manage, despite the forces of modern life working against them, to keep the Test the first river among some handsome equals.